dreamy quilts

14 Timeless Projects to Welcome You Home

Lydia Loretta Nelson

stashBOOKS.

an imprint of C&T Publishing

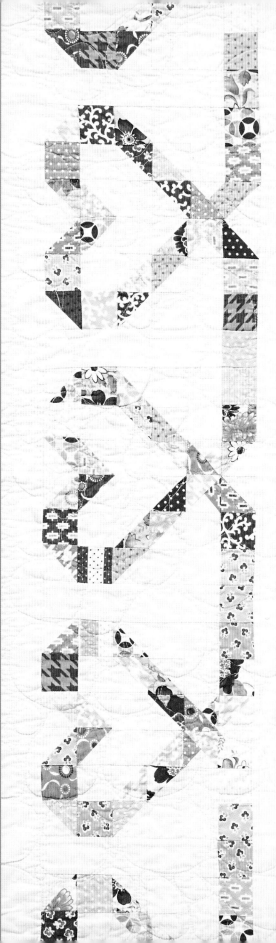

Text and photography copyright © 2015 by Lydia Loretta Nelson

Photography and artwork copyright © 2015 by C&T Publishing, Inc.

Publisher: Amy Marson

Creative Director: Gailen Runge

Art Director: Kristy Zacharias

Editor: Monica Gyulai

Technical Editors: Debbie Rodgers and Julie Waldman

Cover/Book Designer: April Mostek

Production Coordinator: Zinnia Heinzmann

Production Editor: Katie Van Amburg

Illustrator: Aliza Shalit

Photo Assistant: Mary Peyton Peppo

Photo Stylist: Lauren Toker

Style photography by Nissa Brehmer and
instructional photography by Diane Pedersen, unless otherwise noted

Published by Stash Books, an imprint of C&T Publishing, Inc.,
P.O. Box 1456, Lafayette, CA 94549

Library of Congress Cataloging-in-Publication Data

Nelson, Lydia Loretta, 1984-

Dreamy quilts : 14 timeless projects to welcome you home / Lydia Loretta
Nelson.

    pages cm

ISBN 978-1-61745-028-0 (soft cover)

1. Quilts. 2. Quilting--Patterns. 3. House furnishings. I. Title.

TT835.N443 2015

746.46--dc23

                                    2014033384

Printed in China

10 9 8 7 6 5 4 3 2 1

Contents

dedication

To my darling husband, Tony, who always believes in me. You are my best friend and the absolute love of my life.

Photo by Scottie Magro

acknowledgments

Thank you to my husband, Tony, for supporting my artistic endeavors, whether this means encouraging me to take a night class in graphic design, buying me a new sewing machine, or paying no mind to the fabric and threads that festoon our house. Thank you to my three beautiful boys for sparking creativity in me. To my parents, for all things big and small that parenthood requires … and for doing it with so much love. To C&T, for breathing fresh air into the world of quilting and sewing and for believing in my vision.

Photo by Lydia Nelson

introduction

Welcome to *Dreamy Quilts*! The idea for this book evolved from my combined passion for quilting and interior design. I use quilts to satisfy my craving for a unique home.

My family used to move often because my husband was in the military for 11½ years. Together with our three sons, we lived on military posts where the homes themselves were quite generic. I made them "ours" by carefully selecting the paint colors, furniture, linens, throw pillows, framed art, photography, and, of course, quilts that filled the rooms.

Draping a new quilt over a sofa can add a fresh look to any home, as can hanging a quilt on the wall of a drab apartment. Even a dorm room or a long-stay hotel takes on your personality when you add a handmade element. And the bonus is that you're not committed permanently. You can make new quilts to suit your evolving taste or the seasons and swap them out effortlessly no matter where you live.

That approach to decorating is the idea behind this book—dreamy patterns for a dreamy home.

My idea of a dreamy quilt is a quilt that is soft and soothing to the eyes, with a palette drawn from nature. It is a quilt that is not overly complicated by an abundance of prints and colors. When I spend hours making a quilt, I don't want the print of the fabrics to be the focus. Instead, I want the patchwork and piecing detail to stand out. The key to achieving a dreamy quilt is to choose just one or two main prints for your quilt and select coordinating solids and neutrals for the remaining fabrics.

I hope you will make these quilts your own. Switch out white fabric for a crisp buttercream or pastel batik. Customize the size of your quilt by adding a border or subtracting a row of blocks.

With all this in mind, have fun picking out fabric for your next project and don't try to cram tons of prints into one quilt. Make the most elegant quilt you've ever dreamed of.

getting started

tools of the trade

Quilting, like all hobbies, requires a few essential tools. Buy the best quality you can afford and they will last longer and perform better. For example, I notice a huge difference in the neatness of my cutting lines when I use an Olfa rotary cutter instead of a thrifty off-brand one. Here are some essential tools you need to get started.

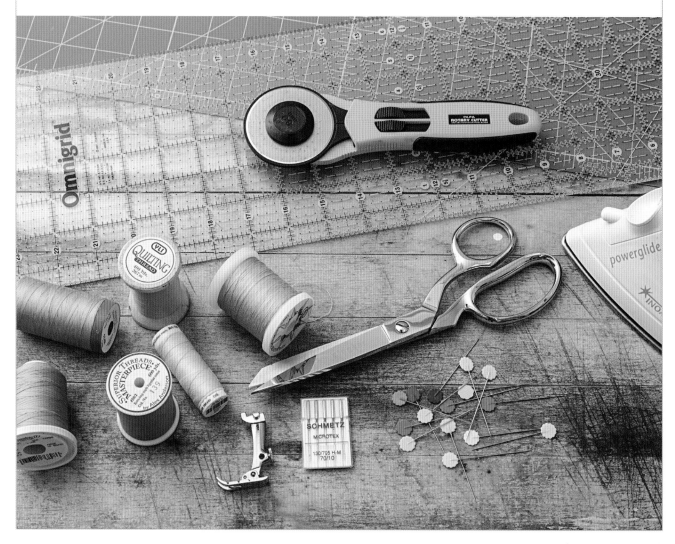

Thread and Needles

For both piecing and quilting I recommend 100% cotton thread. Piecing is best with 50-weight thread, and quilting is best with slightly heavier 40-weight thread. I use a 70/10 microtex needle, which is a sharp midsized needle. Be diligent and change your needle regularly—at least once per project.

Rotary Cutter

Rotary cutters come in a variety of sizes from 18mm to 60mm and are indispensable to quilters. I use my 60mm Olfa cutter most frequently and change the blade at least once per project. As the blade dulls it can drag on the fabric and fail to cut straight, neat lines.

Rulers

Most quilters use a wide assortment of rulers while working. If you are just getting started and only buy one, start with a 6″ × 24″ Omnigrid Quilter's Ruler. The 24″ length makes it ideal for cutting strips from standard-width fabric folded in half.

Cutting Mat

Rotary cutting requires a trio of tools that work together. A self-healing cutting mat is the final tool in the arsenal. The bigger the better, though bear in mind the size of your table. A mat that measures 24″ × 36″ is good to have.

¼″ Piecing Foot

Not all sewing machines come with a ¼″ piecing foot, but it's a really important tool for quilters. The standard quilt seam allowance is ¼″, and a foot designed for quilting allows you to align the edges of your fabric with the edge of the foot. I recommend investing in a ¼″ piecing foot if you don't have one. However, a piece of painter's tape placed on your machine's throat plate ¼″ to the right of the needle will work too.

Pins

My absolute favorite pins are flower-head pins, sold under various brands. The flowers on the ends of these pins make them easy to grab and easy to spot when they fall on the floor.

Iron

Investing in a heavy-duty iron is an excellent idea if you will be doing a lot of quilting. A good iron usually costs around $100 but works far better than a $15 iron. My six-year-old Shark is heavy, which makes pressing fabric easy. An added bonus? It has survived the dozens of times I've dropped it on the floor!

Scissors

Quilters need at least one good pair of scissors that is reserved only for cutting fabric. You will use yours for everything from snipping corners to trimming frayed fabric. Don't let fabric scissors find their way into little hands for craft projects. Glue and fabric are a bad combo!

prepping fabric

Prewashing

I generally do not prewash my fabric unless it is highly pigmented (think solid reds or blues) and will likely bleed when the quilt is later washed. If you decide to prewash, allot some extra time for pressing and trimming. Washed fabric becomes wrinkled and the cut ends unravel, requiring lots of snipping.

Pressing

Begin by pressing your fabric. Open it up and press out any wrinkles and fold lines. Use an up-and-down motion and push the steam button frequently. Do not drag your iron back and forth across the fabric.

Squaring Up

Squaring up fabric perfectly takes some practice, but it is an important step. If the lengthwise and crosswise threads in the fabric are not perpendicular, the edges of straight-cut pieces can stretch and distort. Here are the basics:

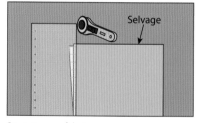

Squaring up fabric

1. After pressing, align the selvages on a horizontal line on your cutting mat. Shift the top layer of the fabric right or left so that it lies flat and the selvage ends line up perfectly. Do not expect the cut ends of your fabric to line up too. They will be trimmed.

2. Align a clear, gridded ruler with the horizontal lines on the cutting mat and trim off enough from a cut end to get a clean edge. Afterward, cut a small test strip about 1″ in width and check whether the strip is straight or crooked, especially where it was folded in half on the bolt. If the strip is wavy, square up the fabric again. This is a very important step. Perfect squaring up allows for perfectly cut pieces.

dreamy color schemes

Personalize your quilts by choosing fabrics and colors that suit your style. It's amazing how dramatically the look of a quilt changes when you swap one fabric for another.

For the dreamy look, use only one or two patterned fabrics together with neutral solids. Or, use a variety of patterned fabrics but keep the block backgrounds and sashing neutral. This approach makes for quilts that are soft on the eyes—delicate and light.

In addition to their quiet aesthetic, dreamy quilts complement the decor in most homes. And piecing details stand out because they aren't competing with an abundance of patterned fabric.

Here's a lesson in going neutral. Look at these fabric groupings. Each features just one quiet pattern together with solids.

The same quilt design looks very different when different fabrics are used. The following two sets of three quilts have each been recolored to demonstrate the difference a color shift can make. The first one in each set displays the palettes used for projects in *Dreamy Quilts*. It's followed by a version using bolder hues and several colors. The third variation was recolored with fewer, softer colors. The middle quilts have a busier feel even though the quilt designs are exactly the same.

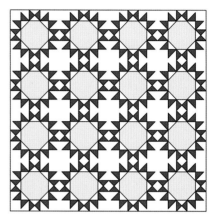

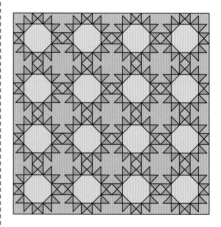

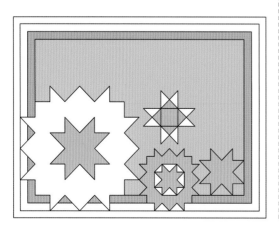

dreamy projects

greta goose

Finished Block: 15″ × 15″ • **Finished Quilt:** 55″ × 55″

Adorned with lace and vintage linen appliqué, *Greta Goose* would look beautiful draped over a crib, on a wall, or in baby portraits. It's composed of three different blocks: a center medallion, an Eight-Point Star, and a goose appliqué. The fabric requirements are given for the entire quilt, but cutting and piecing will be done one block at a time.

MATERIALS

WHITE: 1⅝ yards

RED PRINT: 1 yard

BUTTERCREAM: ⅜ yard

KHAKI: 1⅝ yards

VINTAGE LINEN: 4 pieces
10″ × 10″ for goose appliqués

BACKING: 3½ yards

BIAS BINDING: ⅞ yard neutral fabric

BATTING: 63″ × 63″

LACE TRIM: 7 yards

FUSIBLE WEB: ½ yard

TIP: Garage sales, flea markets, and Etsy are great places to find vintage linens. Position your appliqué templates on the vintage linen to showcase fabric designs.

Sew with right sides together and ¼″ seam allowances. Refer to Half-Square Triangles (page 102), Flying Geese (page 103), Appliqué (page 103), and Continuous Bias Binding (page 107) for extra guidance.

CUTTING

WHITE

Cut 3 strips 8″ × width of fabric; subcut into 12 squares 8″ × 8″.

Cut 5 strips 4¼″ × width of fabric; subcut into 36 squares 4¼″ × 4¼″ and 8 rectangles 4¼″ × 2⅜″.

Cut 1 strip 2¾″ × width of fabric; subcut into 4 squares 2¾″ × 2¾″ and 8 squares 2⅜″ × 2⅜″.

RED PRINT

Cut 5 strips 4½″ × width of fabric for borders.

Cut 1 strip 2¾″ × width of fabric; subcut into 8 squares 2¾″ × 2¾″.

Cut 1 strip 2⅜″ × width of fabric; subcut into 4 rectangles 2⅜″ × 4¼″ and 8 squares 2⅜″ × 2⅜″.

BUTTERCREAM

Cut 1 strip 4¼″ × width of fabric; subcut into 1 square 4¼″ × 4¼″, 4 squares 2¾″ × 2¾″, and 4 squares 2⅜″ × 2⅜″.

Cut 5 strips 1¼″ × width of fabric for borders.

CUTTING continued on page 14

Designed and pieced by Lydia Nelson, quilted by Melanie Simpson

CUTTING continued

KHAKI

Cut 2 strips 15½″ × width of fabric; subcut into 4 squares 15½″ × 15½″ and 7 squares 4¼″ × 4¼″.

Cut 4 strips 4¼″ × width of fabric; subcut into 16 rectangles 4¼″ × 8″.

Cut 1 strip 4¼″ × width of fabric; subcut into 9 squares 4¼″ × 4¼″.

VINTAGE LINEN

Use the goose pattern (page 19) and refer to Appliqué (page 103) to make the goose appliqués.

TIP: If the linen has a pattern, arrange the goose shape on it to take advantage of the design.

center medallion

Creation

1. Pair a red 2¾″ × 2¾″ square with a butter-cream 2¾″ × 2¾″ square to make 2 half-square triangles. Make 8. *figure A*

2. Pair a red 2¾″ × 2¾″ square with a white 2¾″ × 2¾″ square to make 2 half-square triangles. Make 8. *figure B*

3. Pair a red 2⅜″ × 4¼″ rectangle with 2 white 2⅜″ × 2⅜″ squares to make a Flying Geese Y unit. Make 4. *figure C*

4. Pair a white 2⅜″ × 4¼″ rectangle with 2 red 2⅜″ × 2⅜″ squares to make a Flying Geese Z unit. Make 4. *figure D*

Preparing Sub-blocks

1. Sew together 1 each of the half-square triangles from Steps 1 and 2 to make sub-block A. Note the orientation in the center block assembly diagram. Make 4 of each. *figure E*

2. Sew a Flying Geese Y unit to a white 2⅜″ × 4¼″ rectangle to make sub-block B. Make 4. *figure F*

A. Make 8.

B. Make 8.

C. Make 4 Flying Geese Y units.

D. Make 4 Flying Geese Z units.

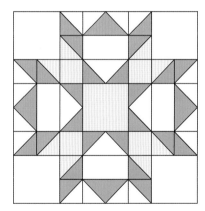

Center block assembly

E. Make 4 each of sub-block A.

F. Make 4 sub-block B.

3. Join sub-blocks A and B to make sub-block C. Make 4. *figure G*

4. Sew 2 buttercream 2⅜″ × 2⅜″ squares to the sides of Flying Geese Z to make sub-block D. Make 2. *figure H*

5. Sew 2 Flying Geese Z units to opposite sides of a 4¼″ × 4¼″ buttercream square to make sub-block E. Make 1. *figure I*

6. Sew together sub-blocks D and E to make an Eight-Point Star. *figure J*

7. Arrange the sub-blocks C from Step 3 around the Eight-Point Star and add 4 white squares 4¼″ × 4¼″ in the corners. Sew together the pieces to complete each row and sew the rows together to form the center block. *figure K*

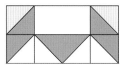

H. Make 2 sub-block D.

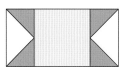

G. Make 4 sub-block C.

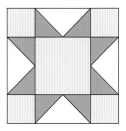

I. Make 1 sub-block E.

J. Eight-Point Star

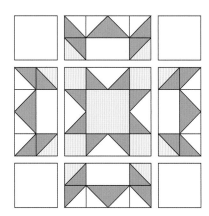

K. Sew rows to complete the block.

goose appliqué block

Creation

Refer to Appliqué (page 103) and Flying Geese (page 103) for extra guidance.

1. On 2 white 8″ × 8″ squares draw a diagonal line on the wrong side between opposite corners. Sew on the drawn lines to the adjacent corners of a khaki 15½″ × 15½″ square. Trim ¼″ away and press open. Make 4.

2. Press the goose appliqué onto the center bottom of each block. Secure using a blanket or zigzag stitch. *figure L*

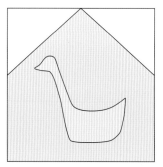

L. Goose block. Make 4.

eight-point star corner block

Creation

1. Pair a khaki 4¼″ × 8″ rectangle with 2 white 4¼″ × 4¼″ squares to make a Flying Geese block. Make 16. *figure M*

M. Make 16 Flying Geese.

2. Lay out 4 khaki 4¼″ × 4¼″ squares, a white 8″ × 8″ square, and 4 Flying Geese. Sew together each row and then sew together the 3 rows to form an Eight-Point Star corner block. Make 4. *figure N*

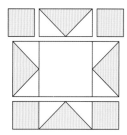

N. Eight-Point Star corner block. Make 4.

quilt top assembly and finishing

Assemble the quilt blocks, as shown in the quilt top layout diagram. Sew together each row and then sew together the 3 rows to complete the quilt top.

Borders

1. Measure the quilt top to determine the length needed for the borders and sew buttercream strips to all 4 sides as instructed in Butted Borders (page 104).

2. Repeat for the red border. *figure O*

Scalloped Edges

Trace the scallop pattern (page 19) and make a template from paper, card stock, or plastic. Use the template to draw the scallop shape with a water-soluble pencil around the red quilt border, smoothing out the lines and corners. *Do not cut yet. figure P*

Quilting and Binding

Refer to Quiltmaking Basics (pages 101–109) for instructions on backing, layering, basting, quilting, trim detailing, and continuous bias binding. After quilting, stitch just inside the scallop lines and then trim just outside the stitching line. Add lace and binding. Press the lace back with the iron to set it in place. Slipstitch the lace to the binding as needed to hold it in place, if desired.

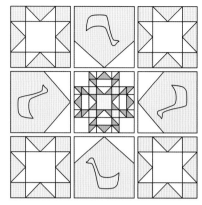

Quilt top layout

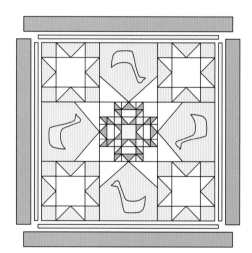

O. Sew 2 sets of borders to quilt sides.

P. Trace scallop shape around quilt.

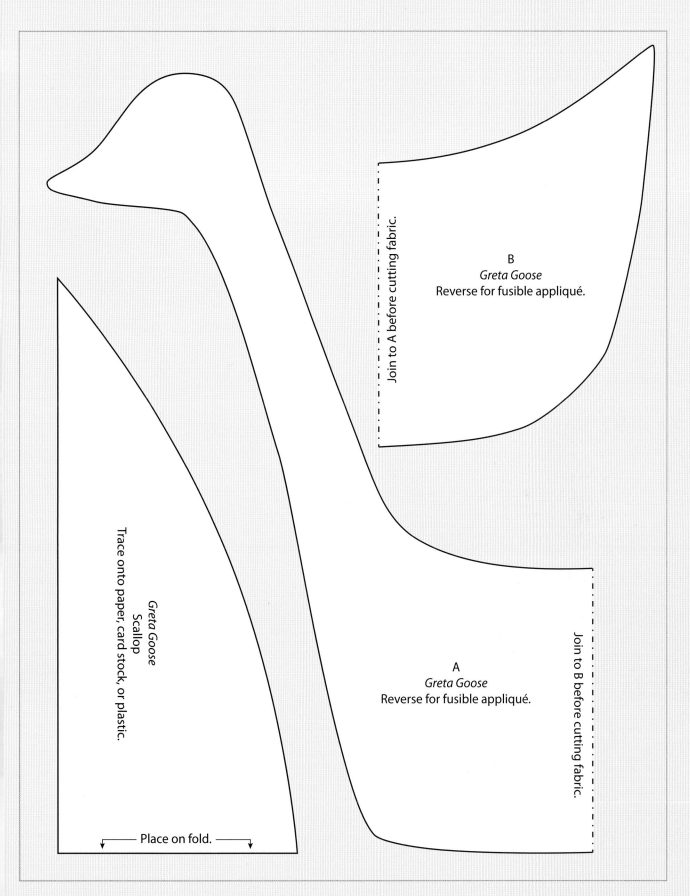

Join to A before cutting fabric.

B
Greta Goose
Reverse for fusible appliqué.

Greta Goose
Scallop
Trace onto paper, card stock, or plastic.

A
Greta Goose
Reverse for fusible appliqué.

Join to B before cutting fabric.

← Place on fold. →

mr. thornhill

Finished Block: 13½″ × 13½″ • **Finished Quilt:** 49″ × 49″

Creative quilting for the guys isn't always easy. Here's a dapper quilt that's original and "mannish" with blocks that showcase the shapes of dress ties. Named after Cary Grant's sharply clad character Mr. Thornhill in Alfred Hitchcock's *North by Northwest*, this stylish quilt is perfect for dashing boys of all sizes.

MATERIALS

WHITE: 2¾ yards

ASSORTED FAT EIGHTHS:
5 for necktie blocks
4 for bow tie blocks

BINDING: ½ yard

BACKING: 3¼ yards

BATTING: 57″ × 57″

CUTTING

Trace the tie patterns (pages 25–27) onto paper, card stock, or plastic to make templates. Label each piece.

WHITE
For the necktie blocks, cut 5 sets of the following.

Cut 1 strip 9″ × width of fabric; subcut pieces below:

Templates A and B: Cut 1 of each and 1 of each reversed.

Cut 2 rectangles 2½″ × 5¼″ (E).

Cut 2 squares 2½″ × 2½″ (G).

Cut 1 rectangle 1½″ × 14″ (H).

Cut 1 rectangle 2⅜″ × 14″ (I).

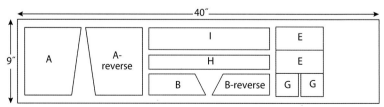

Cutting for necktie block

CUTTING continued on page 22

Photo by Lydia Nelson

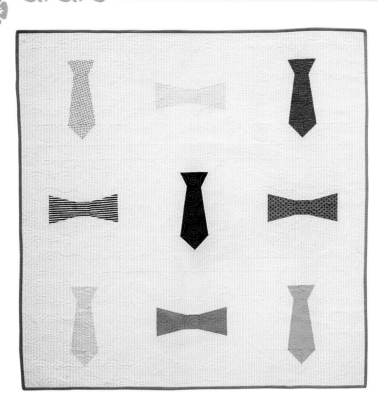

Designed and pieced by Lydia Nelson, quilted by Melanie Simpson

CUTTING continued

WHITE continued

For the bow tie blocks, cut 4 sets of the following.

Cut 1 strip 8″ × width of fabric; subcut pieces below:

Template Y: Cut 2 and 2 reversed.

Cut 2 rectangles 2¼″ × 14″ (U).

Cut 2 rectangles 2½″ × 6¼″ (V).

Cut 8 strips 2½″ × width of fabric; subcut into 6 rectangles 2½″ × 14″. Set aside the rectangles and remaining strips for sashing.

FAT EIGHTHS

For the neckties, from each of 5 fat eighths:

Templates C and D: Cut 1 of each.

Cut 1 rectangle 2½″ × 4½″ (F).

For the bow ties, from each of 4 fat eighths:

Template W: Cut 2.

Cut 1 square 2½″ × 2½″ (X).

BINDING

Cut 6 strips 2½″ × width of fabric.

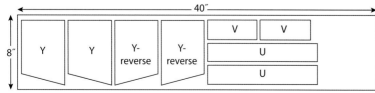

Cutting for bow tie block

creation

Sew with right sides together and ¼˝ seam allowances. Refer to Flying Geese (page 103) for extra guidance and Butted Borders (page 104) for additional information on attaching sashing.

Necktie Blocks

1. Sew together B, D, and B-reverse to form a row.

2. Sew together A, C, and A-reverse to form a row.

3. Sew a Flying Geese unit using a fat-eighth F and 2 white G squares.

4. Sew a rectangle E to each side of the Flying Geese unit to form a row.

5. Sew together the rows and add rectangle H to the bottom and rectangle I to the top.

6. Repeat Steps 1–5 to make 5 blocks.

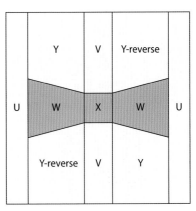

Make 5 necktie blocks.

Bow Tie Blocks

1. Sew together pieces Y, W, and Y-reverse to form a column. Make 2.

2. Sew a rectangle V to either side of square X to form a column.

3. Sew together all the columns and add a rectangle U on either side of the block.

4. Repeat Steps 1–3 to make 4 blocks.

Make 4 bow tie blocks.

sashing

1. Sew 6 sashing strips 2½″ × 14″ between the blocks. *figure A*

2. Piece together 4 sashing strips to equal the width of the quilt. Sew the strips between the rows and to the top and bottom of the quilt. *figure B*

3. Piece together 2 strips to equal the length of the quilt, including the top and bottom sashing. Sew to the right and left sides of the quilt.

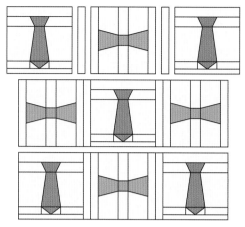

A. Attach short sashing strips to form rows.

quilting and binding

Refer to Quiltmaking Basics (pages 101–109) for instructions on backing, layering, basting, and double-fold straight-grain binding to finish *Mr. Thornhill.*

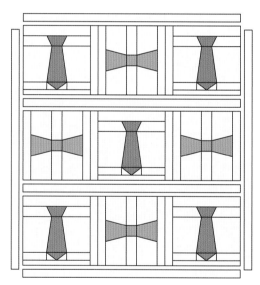

B. Attach long sashing strips.

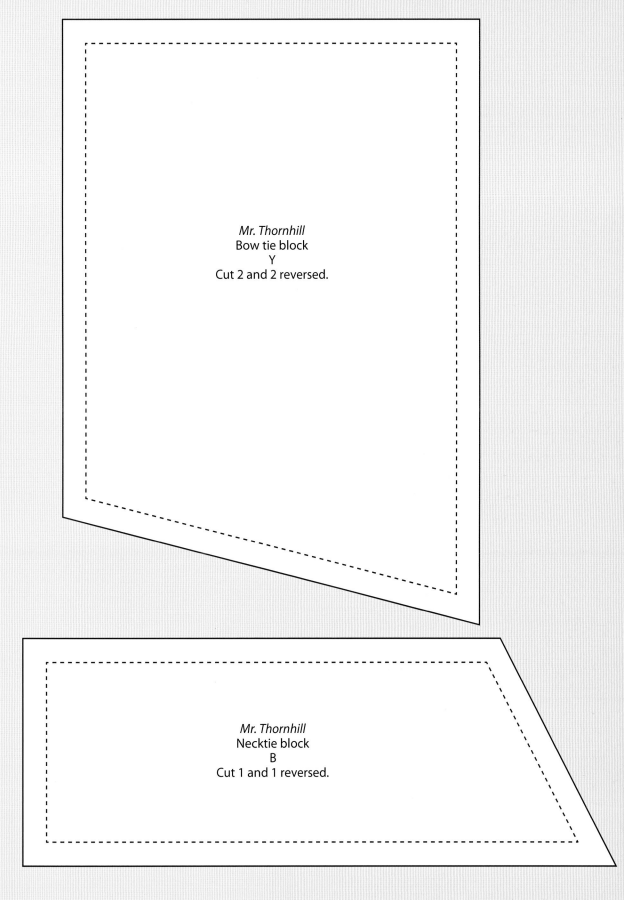

Mr. Thornhill
Bow tie block
Y
Cut 2 and 2 reversed.

Mr. Thornhill
Necktie block
B
Cut 1 and 1 reversed.

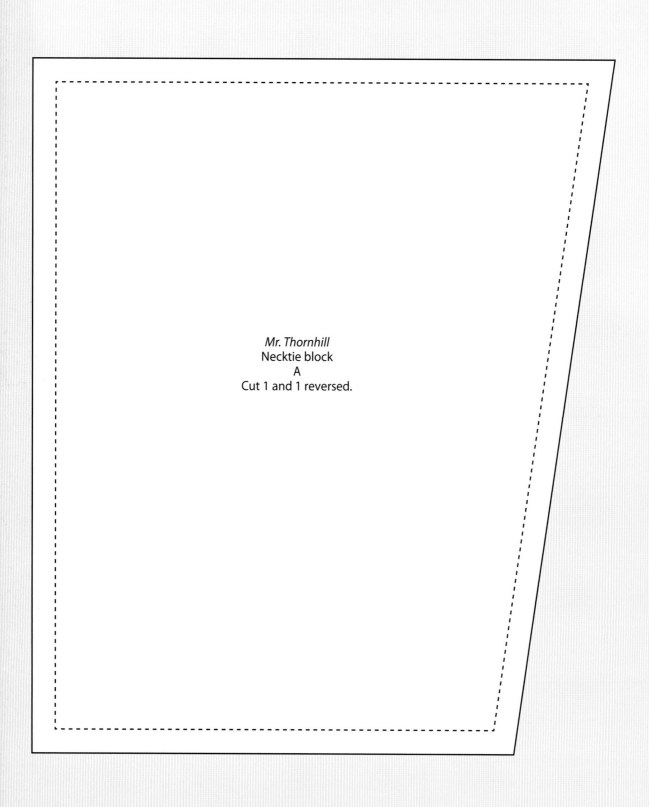

Mr. Thornhill
Necktie block
A
Cut 1 and 1 reversed.

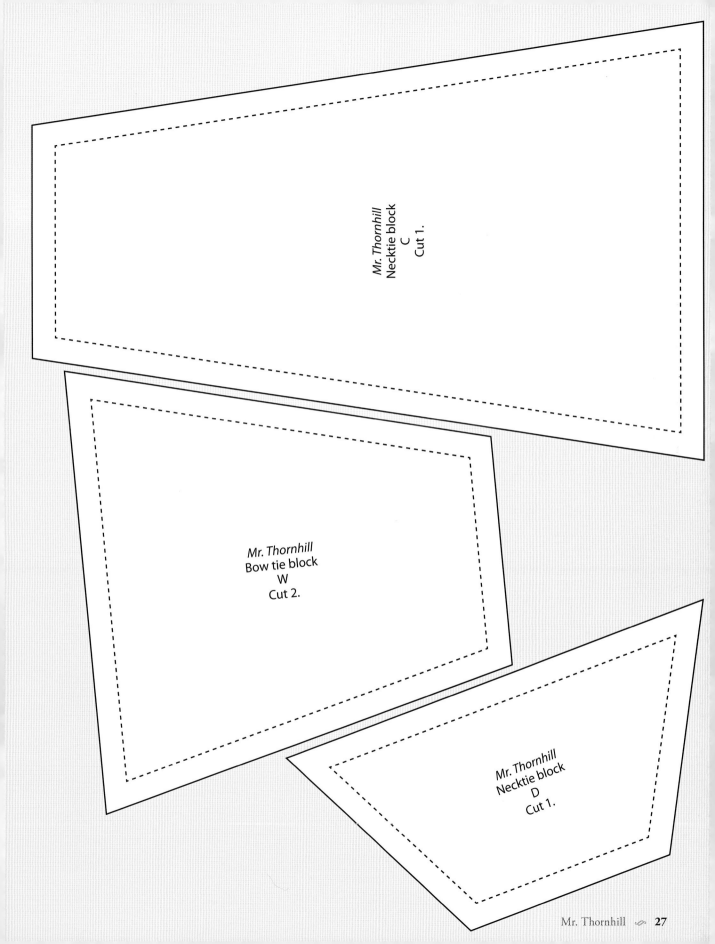

Mr. Thornhill
Necktie block
C
Cut 1.

Mr. Thornhill
Bow tie block
W
Cut 2.

Mr. Thornhill
Necktie block
D
Cut 1.

sweet dreams

Finished Block: 12″ × 18″ • **Finished Quilt:** 58″ × 62″

Peach and white are such a feminine and soft color combination. Sized to be an oversized crib quilt or a right-sized lap quilt, *Sweet Dreams* is suitable for girls both young and grown who desire a touch of elegance.

MATERIALS

WHITE: 3⅛ yards

PEACH SOLID: 1⅜ yards

PEACH PRINT: ⅜ yard

BINDING: ⅝ yard

BACKING: 3¾ yards

BATTING: 66″ × 70″

CUTTING

WHITE

Cut 29 strips 2½″ × width of fabric; subcut into 192 squares 2½″ × 2½″, 48 rectangles 2½″ × 7½″, and 48 rectangles 2½″ × 5½″.

Cut 14 strips 2½″ × width of fabric; subcut 5 into 9 rectangles 2½″ × 18½″. The remaining strips will be pieced for sashing later.

PEACH SOLID

Cut 8 strips 4½″ × width of fabric; subcut into 24 squares 4½″ × 4½″ and 24 rectangles 4½″ × 7½″.

Cut 3 strips 2½″ × width of fabric; subcut into 48 squares 2½″ × 2½″.

PEACH PRINT

Cut 2 strips 4½″ × width of fabric; subcut into 12 squares 4½″ × 4½″.

BINDING

Cut 7 strips 2½″ × width of fabric.

Designed and pieced by Lydia Nelson, quilted by Melanie Simpson

creation

Sew with right sides together and ¼˝ seam allowances. Refer to Sewing Diagonally (page 102) for extra guidance and Butted Borders (page 104) for additional information on attaching sashing.

1. On each peach 4½˝ × 4½˝ square and each peach 4½˝ × 7½˝ rectangle (24 of each), place 2 white 2½˝ × 2½˝ squares on diagonally opposite corners. Sew white squares on the diagonal to the corners. Press and trim.

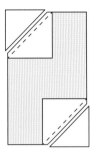
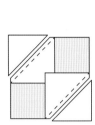

Sew 2 white squares to opposite corners.

2. Sew 2 more 2½˝ × 2½˝ squares to the remaining 2 corners.

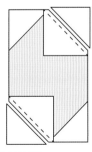
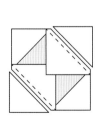

Sew 2 squares to remaining corners.

3. Press and trim.

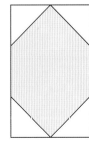
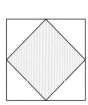

Make 24 of each.

4. Sew together a peach 2½″ × 2½″ square and a white 2½″ × 5½″ rectangle along a short side. Make 48. *figure A*

5. Place the rectangles created in Step 3 so that the peach square is on the bottom and the white rectangle is on top. Sew a white 2½″ × 7½″ rectangle to the left long side of a rectangle. Make 24. Sew a white 2½″ × 7½″ rectangle to the right long side of each remaining piece. Make 24. *figure B*

6. Arrange the pieces following the block piecing diagram with the peach print 4½″ × 4½″ square in the center. Sew together the pieced sections to form 3 columns. Sew the columns together to form a block. Make 12. *figure C*

7. Sew 9 sashing strips 2½″ × 18½″ between the blocks to form the rows.

8. Piece together sashing strips so that they equal the width of the quilt. Sew the strips between the rows and to the top and bottom of the quilt. Measure the length of the quilt and sew the remaining sashing strips end to end to match the quilt length and sew them to the sides. Refer to the instructions for Butted Borders (page 104) for tips on measuring and pinning sashing to strips of blocks. *figure D*

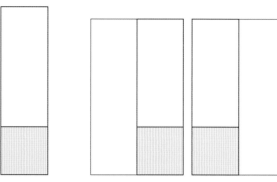

A. Make 48.   B. Make 24 of each.

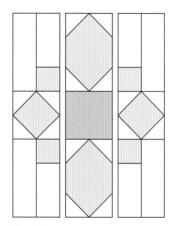

C. Block piecing. Make 12.

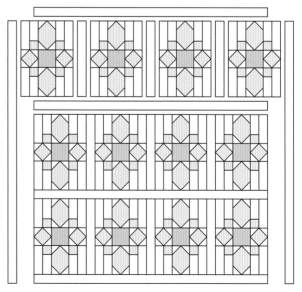

D. Attach sashing.

quilting and binding

Refer to Quiltmaking Basics (pages 101–109) for instructions on backing, layering, basting, and double-fold straight-grain binding to finish *Sweet Dreams*.

hydrangea

Block Size: 15″ × 15″ • **Quilt Size:** 72″ × 72″

Picture an old farmhouse with a big wraparound porch surrounded by lavender hydrangeas. Here's a quilt designed to capture that spirit and reflect the look of those lovely perennials. With an on-point design and alternating dark and light blocks, *Hydrangea* is full of life.

MATERIALS

WHITE: 2½ yards (includes sashing)

GRAY: ¾ yard

BURGUNDY: 1⅞ yards

LAVENDER FLORAL PRINT: 1⅞ yards

BINDING: ⅝ yard

BACKING: 4½ yards

BATTING: 80″ × 80″

Photo by Lydia Nelson

CUTTING

WHITE

Cut 9 strips 4½″ × width of fabric; subcut into 72 squares 4½″ × 4½″. Cut each square in half diagonally to yield 2 right triangles. Make 144.

Cut 18 strips 2½″ × width of fabric; subcut 9 strips into 16 rectangles 2½″ × 15½″ and 2 rectangles 2½″ × 18″. These and the remaining strips will be used later for sashing.

GRAY

Cut 23 strips 2½″ × width of fabric; subcut into 360 squares 2½″ × 2½″. (Stack and cut 3 strips at a time and the job will go by quicker than you may think!)

BURGUNDY

Cut 8 strips 7⅛″ × width of fabric; subcut into 36 squares 7⅛″ × 7⅛″.

LAVENDER FLORAL PRINT

Cut 8 strips 7⅛″ × width of fabric; subcut into 36 squares 7⅛″ × 7⅛″.

BINDING

Cut 8 strips 2½″ × width of fabric.

Photo by Lydia Nelson

Designed and pieced by Lydia Nelson, quilted by Kathy Olkowski

creation

*Sew with right sides together and ¼˝ seam
allowances. Refer to Sewing Diagonally (page 102)
for pointers on making triangles out of squares.*

Triangles

1. Sew a gray 2½˝ × 2½˝ square to the right-angle
corner of a white triangle. Trim the seam to ¼˝ and
press open. Make 144. *figure A*

2. Sew together 60 pairs of the triangles from
Step 1, matching the seams to form large triangles.
Make 60. There will be 24 remaining small triangles,
which will be used in the half-blocks. *figure B*

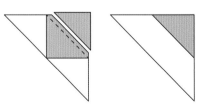

A. Sew gray square to white triangle. Make 144.

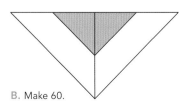

B. Make 60.

Flower Petal Squares

Sew gray 2½″ × 2½″ squares to 3 corners of each burgundy and lavender print 7⅛″ × 7⅛″ square. Trim ¼″ from the seam and press open. Make 36 of each. *figure C*

Assembling the Whole Blocks

1. Using 24 each of the burgundy and lavender print flower petal squares, sew 4 squares together, positioning the gray triangles as shown. Make 6 of each. *figure D*

2. Sew 4 large white/gray triangles to the large square. Center the gray triangles exactly to form a gray square on each side. *figure E*

3. Because the large white/gray triangles are smaller than the large square, there will be an overhang on each corner. Use a ruler and rotary cutter to trim the overhang and make a square that measures 15½″ × 15½″. *figure F*

4. Make 6 whole blocks with burgundy flowers and 6 with lavender print flowers.

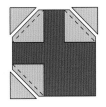

C. Make 36 burgundy and 36 lavender.

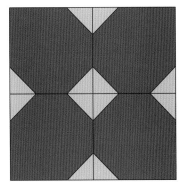

D. Make 6 burgundy and 6 lavender.

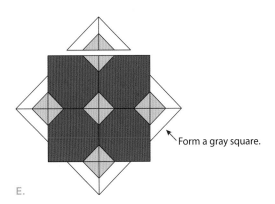

Form a gray square.

E.

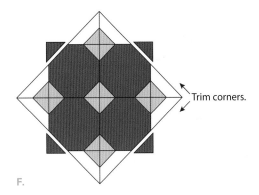

Trim corners.

F.

Assembling the Half-Blocks

1. Using the remaining flower petal squares, sew 2 squares right sides together, forming a rectangle. Position the gray triangles as shown. Press open. Make 6 of each. *figure G*

2. Sew a large white/gray triangle to the rectangle, centering the gray triangle exactly to form a gray square. Sew a small white/gray triangle to each end, matching the gray triangles. *figure H*

3. Because the large white/gray triangles are smaller than the large rectangle, there will be an overhang on each corner. Each trimmed side should measure 15½˝. *figure I*

4. Make 6 half-blocks with burgundy flowers and 6 half-blocks with lavender print flowers.

Sashing

1. Arrange all 24 blocks (12 whole, 12 half) to create an on-point design. Sew a sashing rectangle 2½˝ × 18½˝ between each set of blocks at the upper left and lower right of the quilt, matching the end of the sashing to the edge of the blocks. The other end will be trimmed later.

2. Sew the remaining sashing rectangles 2½˝ × 15½˝ between the other blocks.

G. Make 6 burgundy and 6 lavender.

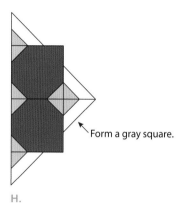

Form a gray square.

H.

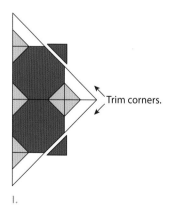

Trim corners.

I.

3. Sew the remaining 9 strips of sashing fabric together end to end. Measure across the center diagonal. Add 2″ and cut 1 strip this length (should be 102½″). Measure the length of the shorter side of the row with 4 whole blocks and 2 half-blocks and add 2″. Cut 2 strips this length (should be 72½″). Measure the shorter side of the row with 2 whole blocks and 2 half-blocks and add 2″. Cut 2 strips this length (should be 38½″).

4. Sew the sashing strips between the rows, and trim the ends even with the edges and corners.

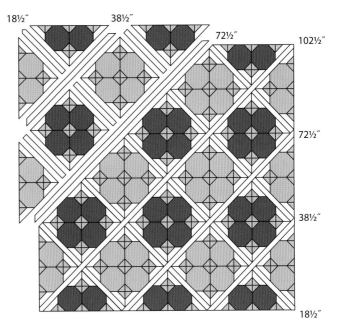

Sew sashing between rows.

quilting and binding

Refer to Quiltmaking Basics (pages 101–109) for instructions on backing, layering, basting, quilting, and double-fold straight-grain binding to finish *Hydrangea*.

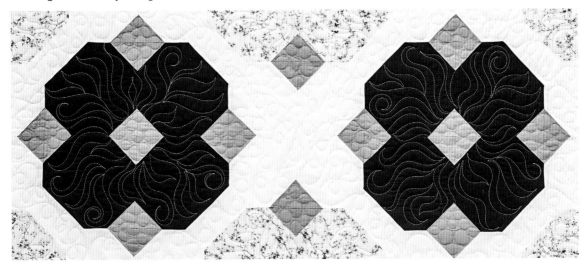

poinsettia

Finished Block: 15″ × 15″ • **Finished Quilt:** 64½″ × 49½″

Poinsettia fills the need for a quilt that's not symmetrical or evenly spaced. With beautiful blocks bursting out of the corner and vintage linen appliqué adding charm, this quilt really stands out, just like the plant it's named after. A red-and-white palette gives *Poinsettia* a classic holiday feel.

MATERIALS

WHITE: 2¾ yards

BROWN: ⅝ yard for border

RED PRINT FOR BLOCKS 1–4: ⅞ yard

RED SOLID FOR BLOCKS 1–4: ⅜ yard

RED PRINT #1 FOR BLOCK 5: 1 fat eighth

RED PRINT #2 FOR BLOCK 5: 1 square 5″

RED PRINT FOR BLOCK 6: ⅜ yard

RED SOLID FOR BLOCK 6: ⅛ yard

RED PRINT FOR BLOCK 7: ¼ yard

APPLIQUÉ: 2 fat quarters

LIGHT FUSIBLE WEB: ½ yard

8″ ROUND VINTAGE LINEN (*OPTIONAL*)

BINDING: ⅝ yard

BACKING: 3¼ yards

BATTING: 72″ × 57″

This entire quilt is pieced before the flower appliqués are added. It is not assembled like most quilts; cutting will be done block by block. Follow the directions carefully. Sew with right sides together and ¼″ seam allowances.

CUTTING BLOCKS 1–4

WHITE

Cut 2 strips 2⅜″ × width of fabric; subcut into 8 rectangles 2⅜″ × 4¼″, 3 rectangles 2⅜″ × 8″, and 1 rectangle 2⅜″ × 6⅛″.

Cut 1 strip 4⅝″ × width of fabric; subcut into 2 squares 4⅝″ × 4⅝″.

Cut 1 strip 4¼″ × width of fabric; subcut into 1 rectangle 4¼″ × 8″ and 7 squares 4¼″ × 4¼″.

BROWN

Cut 2 strips 2⅜″ × width of fabric; subcut into 8 squares 2⅜″ × 2⅜″, 2 rectangles 2⅜″ × 8″, 1 rectangle 2⅜″ × 6⅛″, and 1 rectangle 2⅜″ × 4¼″. (Save the scraps for later.)

RED PRINT

Cut 3 strips 4⅝″ × width of fabric; subcut into 2 squares 4⅝″ × 4⅝″, 4 rectangles 4¼″ × 9⅞″, and 4 rectangles 4¼″ × 11¾″.

Cut 2 strips 2⅜″ × width of fabric; subcut into 4 rectangles 2⅜″ × 4¼″ and 8 squares 2⅜″ × 2⅜″.

Cut 1 strip 8″ × width of fabric; subcut into 4 squares 8″ × 8″.

RED SOLID

Cut 2 strips 4¼″ × width of fabric; subcut into 12 squares 4¼″ × 4¼″.

Designed and pieced by Lydia Nelson, quilted by Kathy Olkowski
Quilt displayed vertically to better show lace details.

Preparing Blocks 1–4

Use sticky notes to label the pieces as indicated in the diagram before assembling the blocks. Refer to Half-Square Triangles (page 102) and Sewing Diagonally (page 102) for extra guidance.

1. Pair a white 4⅝″ × 4⅝″ square with a red print 4⅝″ × 4⅝″ square to make 2 half-square triangles. Make 4 total and label them A. *figure A*

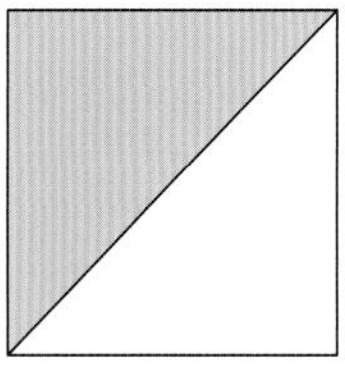

A. Make 4 A units.

2. Sew a white 4¼″ × 4¼″ square to the left side of a red print 4¼″ × 11¾″ rectangle along the diagonal line and sew a solid red 4¼″ × 4¼″ square to the right side along the diagonal line. Trim the seams to ¼″ and press. Make 2 and label them B. *figure B*

B. Make 2 B units.

3. Sew a white 4¼″ × 4¼″ square to the right side of a red print 4¼″ × 11¾″ rectangle on the diagonal and sew a red solid 4¼″ × 4¼″ square to the left side on the diagonal. Trim the seams to ¼″ and press. Make 2 and label them C. *figure C*

C. Make 2 C units.

4. Sew a brown 2⅜″ × 2⅜″ square to the upper left corner of a red print 4¼″ × 9⅞″ rectangle on the diagonal and sew a red solid 4¼″ × 4¼″ square to the right side on the diagonal. Trim the seams to ¼″ and press. Make 2 and label them D. *figure D*

D. Make 2 D units.

5. Sew a red solid 4¼″ × 4¼″ square to the left side of a red print 4¼″ × 9⅞″ rectangle on the diagonal and sew a brown 2⅜″ × 2⅜″ square to the right side on the diagonal. Trim the seams to ¼″ and press. Make 2 and label them E. *figure E*

E. Make 2 E units.

6. Sew a brown 2⅜″ × 2⅜″ square to the left side of a red print 2⅜″ × 4¼″ rectangle on the diagonal. Trim the seam to ¼″ and press. Make 2 and label them F. *figure F*

F. Make 2 F units.

7. Sew a brown 2⅜″ × 2⅜″ square to the right side of a red print 2⅜″ × 4¼″ rectangle on the diagonal. Trim the seam to ¼″ and press. Make 2 and label them G. *figure G*

G. Make 2 G units.

8. Sew a red print 2⅜″ × 2⅜″ square to the left side of a white 2⅜″ × 4¼″ rectangle on the diagonal. Trim the seam to ¼″ and press. Make 4 and label them H. *figure H*

H. Make 4 H units.

9. Sew a red print 2⅜″ × 2⅜″ square to the right side of a white 2⅜″ × 4¼″ rectangle on the diagonal. Trim the seam to ¼″ and press. Make 4 and label them I. *figure I*

I. Make 4 I units.

Block 1 Creation

TIP: Pay close attention: This block is a little tricky. Lay out the parts before piecing, if necessary.

1. Sew together H, E, and a solid red 4¼″ × 4¼″ square to form row 1.

2. Sew together I and G. Sew a white 2⅜″ × 6⅛″ rectangle to a brown 2⅜″ × 6⅛″ rectangle. Sew I/G to this rectangle, as in the diagram.

3. Sew a brown 2⅜″ × 4¼″ rectangle to F. Sew to the 8″ × 8″ red print square.

4. Sew the sets from Steps 2 and 3 with D to form row 2.

5. Sew together a white 2⅜″ × 8″ rectangle, H, and I to form row 3.

6. Sew together rows 1, 2, and 3 to form Block 1. *figure J*

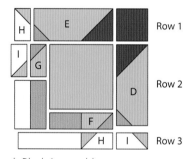

J. Block 1 assembly

Block 2 Creation

1. Sew a white 2⅜″ × 8″ rectangle to a brown 2⅜″ × 8″ rectangle. Sew together H and F. Sew these 2 units together as in the diagram.

2. Sew a white 4¼″ × 4¼″ square to A. Sew to a red print 8″ × 8″ square. Sew this unit to the set from Step 1 and then sew C to the right side to form row 1.

3. Sew together I, D, and a solid red 4¼″ × 4¼″ square to form row 2.

4. Sew together rows 1 and 2 to form Block 2. *figure K*

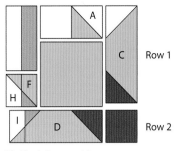

K. Block 2 assembly

Block 3 Creation

1. Sew A to a white 4¼″ × 8″ rectangle. Sew another A to a white 4¼″ × 4¼″ square; then sew to a red print 8″ × 8″ square. Sew these 2 units together and then sew to B to form row 1.

2. Sew a solid red 4¼″ × 4¼″ square to C to form row 2.

3. Sew together rows 1 and 2 to form Block 3. *figure L*

L. Block 3 assembly

Block 4 Creation

1. Sew a solid red 4¼″ × 4¼″ square to B to form row 1.

2. Sew A to a white 4¼″ × 4¼″ square; then sew to the right side of a red print 8″ × 8″ square.

3. Sew G to a brown 2⅜″ × 8″ rectangle. Sew this strip to the bottom of the set made in Step 2. Sew E to the left side to form row 2.

4. Sew together H, I, and a white 2⅜″ × 8″ rectangle to form row 3.

5. Sew together the rows to form Block 4. *figure M*

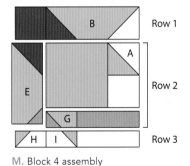

M. Block 4 assembly

CUTTING BLOCK 5

WHITE

Cut 1 strip 5″ × width of fabric; subcut into 1 square 5″ × 5″ and 4 squares 4¼″ × 4¼″.

Cut the 5″ × 5″ square in half diagonally *twice* to yield 4 right triangles.

Cut square in half diagonally twice.

Cut 2 strips 2⅜″ × width of fabric; subcut into 2 rectangles 2⅜″ × 15½″ and 2 rectangles 2⅜″ × 11¾″.

RED PRINT #1 (CENTER BLOCK AND OUTSIDE POINTS)

Cut 2 squares 5″ × 5″ and 1 square 4¼″ × 4¼″.

Cut the 5″ × 5″ squares in half diagonally *twice* to yield 8 right triangles.

RED PRINT #2 (INTERIOR TRIANGLES)

Cut 1 square 5″ × 5″.

Cut the 5″ × 5″ square in half diagonally *twice* to yield 4 right triangles.

block 5 creation

1. Make sub-blocks by assembling 2 triangles from red print #1, a triangle from red print #2, and a triangle from the white fabric in the shape of a square. Sew a white triangle to a red triangle and sew the remaining 2 triangles together. Sew together all the pieces to make a square. Make 4. *figure N*

2. Arrange 4 white squares, the sub-blocks from Step 1, and a red print 4¼″ × 4¼″ square as shown. Sew into 3 rows and then sew together the rows. *figure O*

3. Sew white 2⅜″ × 11¾″ rectangles to the sides; then sew white 2⅜″ × 15½″ rectangles to the top and bottom to complete Block 5. *figure P*

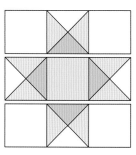

N. Make 4 sub-blocks.

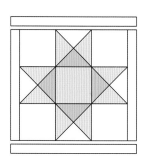

O.

P. Block 5 assembly

BLOCK 6 CUTTING

WHITE

Cut 2 strips 2⅜″ × width of fabric; subcut into 10 squares 2⅜″ × 2⅜″ and 4 rectangles 2⅜″ × 4¼″.

Cut 1 strip 2¾″ × width of fabric; subcut into 4 squares 2¾″ × 2¾″.

BROWN

Cut 2 squares 2⅜″ × 2⅜″ from scraps set aside earlier.

RED PRINT

Cut 1 strip 4¼″ × width of fabric; subcut into 5 squares 4¼″ × 4¼″.

Cut 1 strip 2⅜″ × width of fabric; subcut into 8 rectangles 2⅜″ × 4¼″.

Cut 1 strip 2¾″ × width of fabric; subcut into 4 squares 2¾″ × 2¾″ and 8 squares 2⅜″ × 2⅜″.

RED SOLID

Cut 1 strip 2⅜″ × width of fabric; subcut into 4 squares 2⅜″ × 2⅜″ and 4 rectangles 2⅜″ × 4¼″.

block 6 creation

1. Sew together a white 2¾″ × 2¾″ square and a red print 2¾″ × 2¾″ square along both sides of the diagonal to make 2 half-square triangles. Trim the seams to ¼″ and press open. Make 8. *figure Q*

2. Sew a solid red 2⅜″ × 2⅜″ square to 1 corner of a red print 4¼″ × 4¼″ square. Trim the seam to ¼″ and press open. Make 4. *figure R*

3. Sew 2 white 2⅜″ × 2⅜″ squares to a red print 2⅜″ × 4¼″ rectangle to make a Flying Geese unit. Make 4. *figure S*

4. Sew 2 red print 2⅜″ × 2⅜″ squares to a solid red 2⅜″ × 4¼″ rectangle to make a Flying Geese unit. Make 4. *figure T*

Note: Make the following sub-blocks using half-square triangles from Step 1.

5. Sew a white 2⅜″ × 4¼″ rectangle to the right side of a half-square triangle. Make 2. *figure U*

6. Sew a white 2⅜″ × 4¼″ rectangle to the left side of a half-square triangle. Make 2. *figure V*

Q. Make 8.

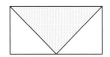

R. Make 4.

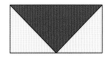

S. Make 4.

T. Make 4.

U. Make 2.

V. Make 2.

7. Sew a white 2⅜″ × 2⅜″ square to the right side of a half-square triangle. *figure W*

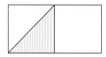

W. Make 1.

8. Sew a white 2⅜″ × 2⅜″ square to the left side of a half-square triangle. *figure X*

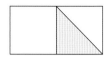

X. Make 1.

9. Sew a brown 2⅜″ × 2⅜″ square to the right side of a half-square triangle. *figure Y*

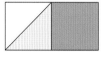

Y. Make 1.

10. Sew a brown 2⅜″ × 2⅜″ square to the left side of a half-square triangle. *figure Z*

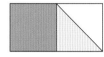

Z. Make 1.

11. Referring to the diagram, arrange all the sub-blocks and remaining 4 red print rectangles 2⅜″ × 4¼″ and the 4¼″ × 4¼″ red print square. Sew them together to form rows and then sew the rows together to complete the block. *figure AA*

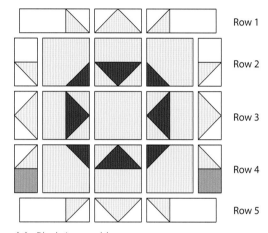

Row 1
Row 2
Row 3
Row 4
Row 5

AA. Block 6 assembly

CUTTING BLOCK 7

WHITE

Cut 1 strip 3⅜″ × width of fabric; subcut into 4 rectangles 3⅜″ × 6⅛″ and 4 squares 3⅜″ × 3⅜″.

Cut 1 strip 2⅜″ × width of fabric; subcut into 1 rectangle 2⅜″ × 13¾″ and 1 rectangle 2⅜″ × 15⅝″.

BROWN

Cut 1 strip 2⅜″ × width of fabric; subcut into 1 rectangle 2⅜″ × 13¾″ and 1 rectangle 2⅜″ × 11⅞″.

RED PRINT

Cut 1 strip 6⅛″ × width of fabric; subcut into 1 square 6⅛″ × 6⅛″ and 8 squares 3⅜″ × 3⅜″.

block 7 creation

1. Sew 2 red print 3⅜″ × 3⅜″ squares to a white 3⅜″ × 6⅛″ rectangle to make a Flying Geese unit. Make 4. *figure BB*

BB. Make 4.

2. Sew 2 white 3⅜″ × 3⅜″ squares to opposite sides of a Flying Geese unit. Make 2.

3. Sew 2 Flying Geese to opposite sides of a red print 6⅛″ × 6⅛″ square.

4. Arrange units from Steps 2 and 3 to form an Eight-Point Star and sew together.

5. Sew a brown 2⅜″ × 11⅞″ rectangle to the right side of the block.

6. Sew a brown 2⅜″ × 13¾″ rectangle to the bottom of the block.

7. Sew a white 2⅜″ × 13¾″ rectangle to the bottom of the block and sew the last white 2⅜″ × 15⅝″ rectangle to the right side to complete Block 7. *figure CC*

Note: Block 7 is ⅛″ larger than the others, so you will need to ease it slightly when sewing it to the adjacent blocks.

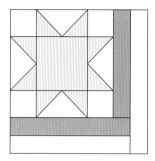

CC. Block 7 assembly

CUTTING REMAINING BLOCKS

WHITE
Cut 1 strip 15½″ × width of fabric; subcut into 3 rectangles 15½″ × 11¾″.

Cut 5 strips 2⅜″ × width of fabric; subcut into 5 rectangles 2⅜″ × 15½″ and 2 rectangles 2⅜″ × 13⅝″.

Cut 1 strip 11¾″ × width of fabric; subcut into 2 squares 11¾″ × 11¾″.

BROWN
Cut 4 strips 2⅜″ × width of fabric; subcut into 3 rectangles 2⅜″ × 15½″, 2 rectangles 2⅜″ × 13⅝″, and 2 rectangles 2⅜″ × 11¾″.

corner and side block creation

1. Sew a brown rectangle 2⅜″ × 11¾″ to the left side of a white square 11¾″ × 11¾″. Sew a brown 2⅜″ × 13⅝″ rectangle to the top.

2. Sew a white 2⅜″ × 13⅝″ rectangle to the top and sew a white 2⅜″ × 15½″ rectangle to the side to make a corner block. Make 2. *figure DD*

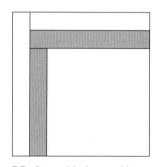

DD. Corner block assembly

3. Sew together a white 2⅜″ × 15½″ rectangle, a brown 2⅜″ × 15½″ rectangle, and a white 11¾″ × 15½″ rectangle to make a side block. Make 3. *figure EE*

EE. Side block assembly

quilt top assembly

Assemble all 12 blocks as shown in the block layout for *Poinsettia*. Sew the blocks together in rows and then sew the rows together. *figure FF*

Appliqué

Use the *Poinsettia* pattern pieces and follow the instructions for Appliqué (page 103) to add flowers to your quilt top. If you are using an 8″ round vintage linen, sew it to the center of the large corner Eight-Point Star and secure it with a blanket or zigzag stitch.

Border

From white fabric, cut 6 strips 2½″ × width of fabric. Stitch the strips together end to end. Attach to the sides, top, and bottom of the quilt following the instructions for Butted Borders (page 104).

Binding

Cut 7 strips 2½″ × width of fabric.

quilting and binding

Refer to Quiltmaking Basics (pages 101–109) for instructions on backing, layering, basting, quilting, and double-fold straight-grain binding to finish *Poinsettia*.

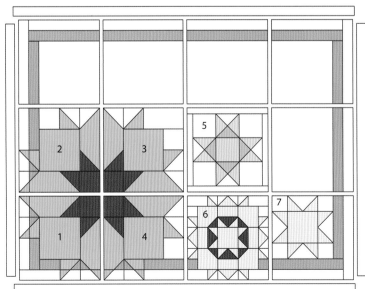

FF. Block layout for *Poinsettia*

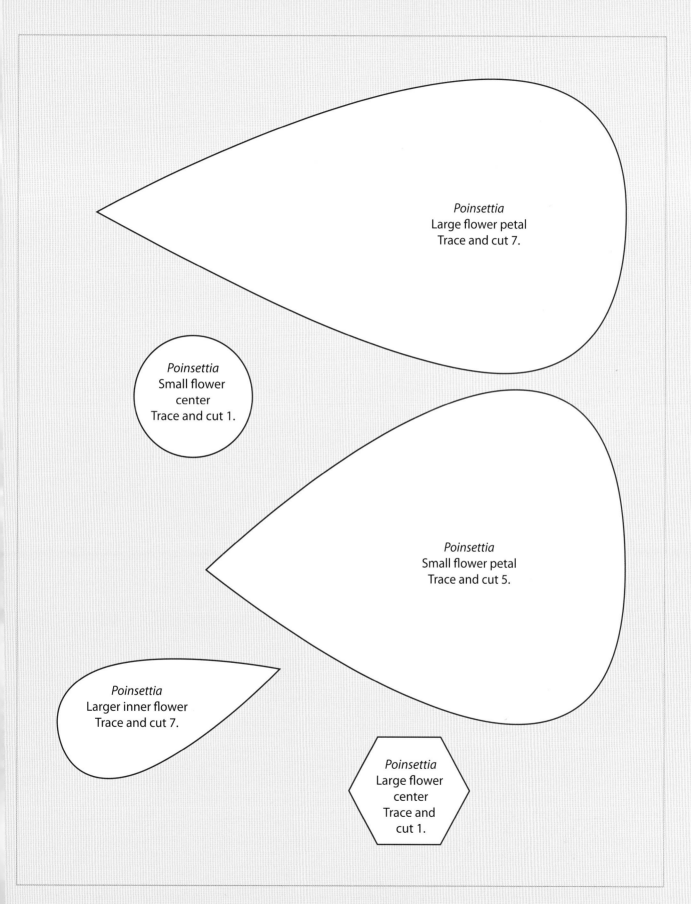

Poinsettia
Large flower petal
Trace and cut 7.

Poinsettia
Small flower
center
Trace and cut 1.

Poinsettia
Small flower petal
Trace and cut 5.

Poinsettia
Larger inner flower
Trace and cut 7.

Poinsettia
Large flower
center
Trace and
cut 1.

signs of spring

Block Size: 13″ × 13″ • **Quilt Size:** 77½″ × 77½″

*S*igns of Spring is inspired by buds in bloom, the smell of freshly cut grass, and the breath of fresh air a new season can bring.

MATERIALS

WHITE: 4⅝ yards

YELLOW: 1⅜ yards

GREEN PRINT: 1⅞ yards

GREEN SOLID: ⅝ yard

BINDING: ¾ yard

BACKING: 7⅛ yards

BATTING: 85″ × 85″

Photo by Lydia Nelson

CUTTING

WHITE

Cut 4 strips 6½″ × width of fabric; subcut into 100 rectangles 6½″ × 1½″.

Cut 10 strips 3½″ × width of fabric; subcut into 100 squares 3½″ × 3½″.

Cut 22 sashing strips 2½″ × width of fabric; subcut into 20 rectangles 2½″ × 13½″. These strips and the remaining strips will be used later for sashing.

Cut 20 strips 2″ × width of fabric; subcut into 400 squares 2″ × 2″.

YELLOW

Cut 5 strips 5″ × width of fabric; subcut into 100 rectangles 5″ × 2″.

Cut 5 strips 3½″ × width of fabric; subcut into 100 rectangles 3½″ × 2″.

GREEN PRINT

Cut 5 strips 6½″ × width of fabric; subcut into 100 rectangles 6½″ × 2″.

Cut 5 strips 5″ × width of fabric; subcut into 100 rectangles 5″ × 2″.

Cut 1 strip 1½″ × width of fabric; subcut into 25 squares 1½″ × 1½″.

GREEN SOLID

Cut 10 strips 2″ × width of fabric; subcut into 100 squares 2″ × 2″.

BINDING

Cut 8 strips 2½″ × width of fabric.

Designed and pieced by Lydia Nelson, quilted by Kathy Olkowski

creation

Sew with right sides together and ¼″ seam allowances. Refer to Sewing Diagonally (page 102) for extra guidance.

1. Sew a white 2″ × 2″ square to the upper right corner of a yellow 2″ × 3½″ rectangle on the diagonal. Trim the seam to ¼″ and press. Make 100 exactly as shown. *figure A*

A. Make 100.

2. Sew a white 2″ × 2″ square to the upper right corner of a green print 2″ × 6½″ rectangle on the diagonal. Trim the seam to ¼″ and press. Make 100 exactly as shown. *figure B*

B. Make 100.

3. Sew a white 2″ × 2″ square to the lower right corner of a yellow 2″ × 5″ rectangle on the diagonal. Trim the seam to ¼″ and press. Make 100 exactly as shown. *figure C*

C. Make 100.

4. Sew a white 2″ × 2″ square to the lower right corner of a green 2″ × 5″ rectangle on the diagonal. Trim the seam to ¼″ and press. Make 100 exactly as shown. *figure D*

D. Make 100.

5. Make a sub-block by sewing a yellow 2″ × 3½″ rectangle to the bottom of a white 3½″ × 3½″ square. Sew a yellow 2″ × 5″ rectangle to the right side. Sew a green print 2″ × 5″ rectangle to the bottom. Sew a green print 2″ × 6½″ rectangle to the right side. *figure E*

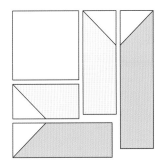

E.

6. Sew a green solid 2″ × 2″ square to a corner of the sub-block on the diagonal. Trim the seam to ¼″ and press open. Make 100. *figure F*

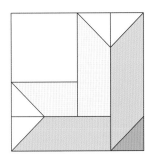

F. Make 100.

7. Sew a green print 1½″ × 1½″ square between 2 white 1½″ × 6½″ rectangles. Make 25. *figure G*

G. Make 25.

8. Sew a white 1½″ × 6½″ rectangle between 2 square sub-blocks. Make 50. *figure H*

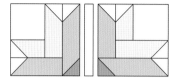

H. Make 50.

9. Sew a rectangle from Step 7 between 2 rectangles from Step 8 to complete the main block. Make 25. *figure I*

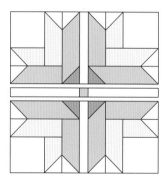

I. Main block assembly. Make 25.

10. Sew 20 sashing rectangles 2½″ × 13½″ between the blocks. Piece together 6 sashing strips to equal the width of the quilt. Sew the strips between the rows and to the top and bottom of the quilt. Piece together 2 sashing strips to equal the length of the quilt and sew them to the sides. Refer to the instructions for Butted Borders (page 104) for tips on measuring and pinning sashing to strips of blocks.

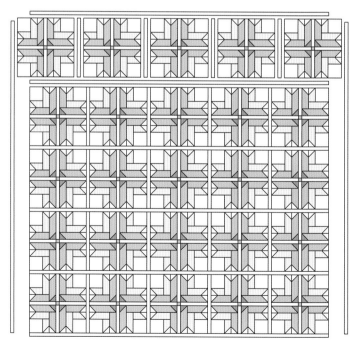

Quilt top layout

quilting and binding

Refer to Quiltmaking Basics (pages 101–109) for instructions on backing, layering, basting, quilting, and double-fold straight-grain binding to finish *Signs of Spring*.

dreamy duvet cover

Finished Block: 23¾" × 23¾" • **Finished King-Size Quilt:** 109¼" × 95½"

Finished Queen-Size Quilt: 95½" × 95½"

Nothing makes a bedroom more romantic than gentle, delicate touches. Based on a traditional Flying Geese block design, the *Dreamy Duvet Cover* can make a bedroom into a serene retreat. Designed to work like a huge pillowcase, it's a pieced cover for a down duvet. Give your senses a rest from the busy world and turn your bed into a cloud. Sweet dreams!

TIP: For a holiday duvet cover, use red and white fabrics. Hang an evergreen wreath above the bed to create a truly festive retreat for chilly winter nights.

MATERIALS

Make this to fit a king- or queen-size duvet. The only difference between the sizes is the addition of sashing around the blocks for the king-size cover.

Note: Use 42"-wide fabric for the white, blue, and print fabrics; otherwise, you will need additional yardage.

WHITE: 7 yards (8¼ yards to include king-size sashing)

BLUE: 4 yards

PRINT: 2½ yards for block centers

DUVET COVER LOOSE BACKING: 3⅛ yards 120"-wide fabric *or* 9⅝ yards 40"-wide fabric

TIES (FOR CLOSING BACK OF DUVET COVER): 2½ yards rickrack or ribbon

BATTING (*OPTIONAL*): 117" × 103" (king) *or* 103" × 103" (queen)

QUILT TOP BACKING (*OPTIONAL*): 116¾" × 103" (king) *or* 103" × 103" (queen)

CUTTING

Cut 25 strips 5¾″ × width of fabric; subcut into 64 squares 5¾″ × 5¾″ and 128 rectangles 5¾″ × 4½″.

Cut 8 strips 4½″ × width of fabric; subcut into 64 squares 4½″ × 4½″.

Cut 20 strips 3⅛″ × width of fabric; subcut into 256 squares 3⅛″ × 3⅛″.

BLUE (POINTS ON THE BLOCKS)

Cut 10 strips 5¾″ × width of fabric; subcut into 128 rectangles 5¾″ × 3⅛″.

Cut 16 strips 4½″ × width of fabric; subcut into 128 squares 4½″ × 4½″.

PRINT (BLOCK CENTERS)

Cut 6 strips 13¾″ × width of fabric; subcut into 16 squares 13¾″ × 13¾″.

SASHING (KING-SIZE DUVET COVER ONLY)

Cut 12 strips 3¼″ × width of fabric.

creation

Sew with right sides together and ¼″ seam allowances. Refer to Sewing Diagonally (page 102) and Flying Geese (page 103) for extra guidance.

1. Pin a white 4½″ × 4½″ square to each corner of a print fabric 13¾″ × 13¾″ square. Sew diagonally, using your favorite method. Trim the seams to ¼″ and press open. Make 16. *figure A*

2. Sew 2 white 3⅛″ × 3⅛″ squares to a blue 3⅛″ × 5¾″ rectangle to make a Flying Geese unit. Make 128. *figure B*

3. Sew a blue 4½″ × 4½″ square diagonally to the upper left corner of a white 4½″ × 5¾″ rectangle. Trim the seam to ¼″ and press open. Make 64. *figure C*

4. Sew a blue 4½″ × 4½″ square diagonally to the upper right upper corner of a white 4½″ × 5¾″ rectangle. Trim the seam to ¼″ and press open. Make 64. *figure D*

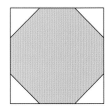

A. Sew 4 squares to corners of print fabric square. Make 16.

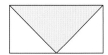

B. Make 128 Flying Geese units.

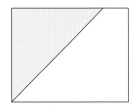

C. Sew blue square to left side of white rectangle. Make 64.

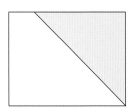

D. Sew blue square to right side of white rectangle. Make 64.

5. Lay out the pieces as shown to form 1 main block, adding the 5¾″ × 5¾″ white squares in the corners. Assemble and sew together the 3 rows. Sew together all the rows to complete a block. Make 16. *figure E*

6. For both quilt sizes, sew together 4 columns of 4 blocks. *figure F*

7. For the king-size duvet cover only, piece together 5 sashing strips to equal the length of the quilt. Sew strips between the columns and on the right and left sides of the quilt. *figure G*

8. For both quilt sizes, sew together all the columns to complete the quilt top.

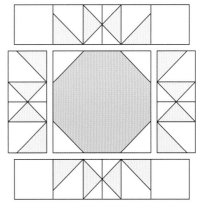

E. Block assembly

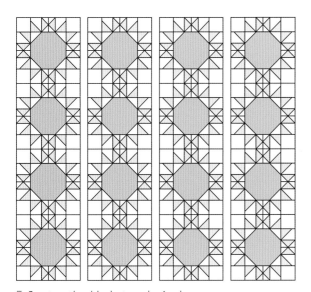

F. Sew together blocks to make 4 columns.

G. Sew sashing between columns for king-size cover.

finishing options

The duvet cover will have a loose backing—it is like a giant pillowcase. But there are several ways of finishing the quilt top itself before sewing it to the loose backing.

- Traditional finish: The top can be treated first like a traditional quilt—with batting, backing, and quilted stitching—and then attached to the loose backing. This approach produces the most "finished" cover and also the warmest.

- Thin finish: Or, the top can be backed with just a layer of fabric so the piecing seams are hidden on the inside of the cover. With this approach, the top can be quilted or not.

- Quick-and-light finish: The last option is to leave the quilted top as is, with raw edges exposed on the inside of the duvet cover. It is the quickest and lightest option.

Choose one of the following finishing options.

Traditional Finish

Quilt the top as normal—either send out the top for quilting or refer to Quiltmaking Basics (pages 101–109) for instructions on backing, layering, basting, and quilting. Once done, proceed to Backing the Duvet Cover (page 63).

TIP: If you send out your top for professional quilting, it may be returned to you with an extra ¼" of backing and batting to add thickness when attaching the binding. Because we are not sewing on binding for this project, ask your machine quilter not to leave the extra ¼", if possible. This will save you from having to trim it off.

Thin Finish

Add a backing to the quilt top and quilt as though there were batting in between. Or, include the backing fabric as a lining to protect the raw piecing seams on the inside of the duvet cover from being abraded. Proceed to the instructions for Backing the Duvet Cover (page 63) without quilting the top lining together.

Quick-and-Light Finish

Simply skip the quilting process altogether and continue to Backing the Duvet Cover (page 63). This easiest and fastest approach to completing a duvet cover is also the least "finished" of the three. You will not have the quilt top quilted to any batting or backing at all. If you were to turn your finished duvet cover inside out, you would see all the raw seams exposed, and that could drive some people crazy.

backing the duvet cover

When completing this last step, just imagine that you are making a giant pillowcase. The pieced top (however you chose to finish it) is like the pillow front, and the backing is the pillow back.

1. If you are not using 120″-wide fabric, you need to piece together the loose backing. (If you are using 120″-wide fabric, skip to Step 2.) Cut 6 pieces 51¼″ × width of fabric and sew 3 pieces together along the long edges. Make 2 and trim to size as in Step 2. The duvet cover backing is in 2 pieces so as to have an opening to insert the duvet.

2. If you are making the king-size duvet cover, cut 2 pieces 109¾″ × 51¼″.

If you are making the queen-size duvet cover, cut 2 pieces 96″ × 51¼″.

3. Turn under a long edge ½″, press, and fold under ½″ again and sew in place ¼″ from the folded edge to hem.

4. Place the finished quilt top face up. Place the 2 backing pieces face down on the quilt top, overlapping the hemmed edges at the center so the backing size matches the quilt top size. There will be a 5″ overlap in the center. *figure H*

5. Pin very well around the edge, every few inches, making sure the overlap is even. Shorten the stitch length on your machine to about 17 stitches per inch and sew around the perimeter. Sew over the ¼″ seam once more to secure. Snip the corners of the duvet cover.

6. Finally, cut the rickrack or ribbon into 10 pieces 8″ long. Divide the 10 pieces of rickrack into 5 pairs. Space them evenly across the overlapping fabric on the back; these will be used to tie together the duvet cover. For the queen size, space them about 16″ apart, and for the king size, space them about 18″ apart. Attach the rickrack by sewing a small square of stitching on the end of each piece, securing the pieces to the duvet cover backing. Place your duvet inside the cover and enjoy! *figure I*

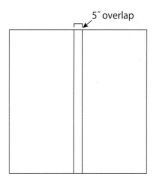

5″ overlap

H. Duvet cover backing

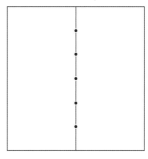

I. Tie placement

candy hearts

Finished Block: 14″ × 12″ • **Finished Quilt:** 84½″ × 51¼″

Here's a quilt inspired by those little boxes of candy hearts that make their appearance around Valentine's Day. *Candy Hearts* is a sweet celebration of the hues and shapes of the holiday, but it will look delicious in your home all year round. Give it a scrappy look using charm packs or a transitional look with ¼-yard cuts.

MATERIALS

WHITE: 3½ yards

HEART BLOCKS: 6 various solids, ¼ yard each *or* 2 charm packs

BINDING: ⅝ yard (You can use leftover heart block fabric if you used solids. Buy an additional ¼ yard.)

BACKING: 5 yards

BATTING: 92″ × 59″

TRIM (*OPTIONAL*): 8 yards

CUTTING

WHITE
Cut 13 strips 2½″ × width of fabric; subcut into 168 squares 2½″ × 2½″ and 6 rectangles 2½″ × 10½″. Set aside the rest of the white fabric for now.

HEART BLOCKS
From ¼-yard cuts: Cut 2 strips 2½″ × width of fabric from each of the 6 colors; subcut into 29 squares 2½″ × 2½″ per color for a total of 174 squares (keep the colors separated).

From charm squares: Cut each square in half twice to yield 4 squares for a total of 174 squares 2½″ × 2½″.

BINDING
Cut 8 strips 2½″ × width of fabric.

Photo by Lydia Nelson

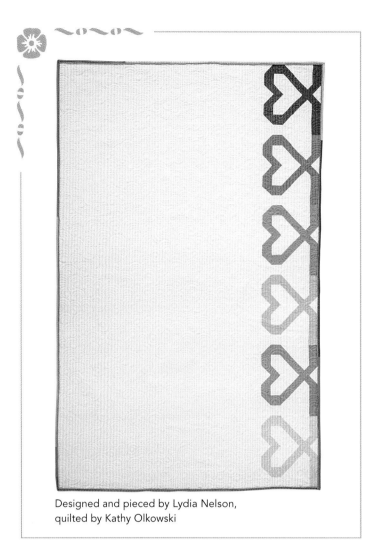

Designed and pieced by Lydia Nelson,
quilted by Kathy Olkowski

creation

Sew with right sides together and ¼˝ seam allowances. Refer to Sewing Diagonally (page 102) for extra guidance.

1. Pair a white 2½˝ × 2½˝ square with a colored 2½˝ × 2½˝ square and sew together on the diagonal to make a half-square triangle. Trim the seam ¼˝ from the sewn line (on either side) and press open. Make 18. *figure A*

2. Take 2 of the white/color squares made in Step 1 and place another color square on top of each. Sew together along the opposite diagonal. Press open. Trim the seam ¼˝ from the sewn line (on either side) and press open. *figure B*

A. Make 18.

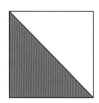

B. Make 2.

3. Lay out the pieces as shown, adding white and color squares. Sew together each row; then sew all the rows to form a heart shape. *figure C*

4. Sew a colored 2½˝ × 2½˝ square to a white 2½˝ × 10½˝ rectangle. Press the seam to 1 side. Sew the unit to the left side of the heart block. *figure D*

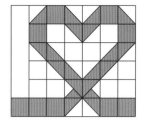

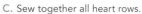

C. Sew together all heart rows.   D. Complete block

5. Repeat Steps 1–4 to complete 6 hearts.

6. Place the heart blocks in the desired order and sew them together, forming a strip of hearts. *figure E*

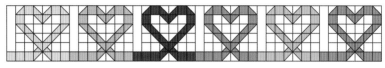

E. Sew together heart blocks.

7. Square up the remaining white fabric and cut the piece so that it matches the length of the heart block strip, which will be about 84½˝. Cut off the selvages and then trim to 39˝ wide, or leave it wider if you prefer to make a slightly bigger quilt. Sew the white fabric piece to the top of the strip of hearts.

quilting and binding

Refer to Quiltmaking Basics (pages 101–109) for instructions on backing, layering, basting, quilting, and double-fold straight-grain binding to finish *Candy Hearts*. Consider adding an optional trim along the quilt's edge before binding, as described in Trim Detailing (page 107).

sweet scarlet

Finished Blocks: 20″ × 20″ and 40″ × 40″ • Finished Quilt: 100″ × 100″

Surely one of life's precious gifts is a nap. Make a midday rest even more special with a star-struck coverlet to keep you warm. And if a nap remains just a distant goal, at least the bed will look good decked out with hues of red.

MATERIALS

Note: The construction of this quilt uses 2 half-square triangles for the large Flying Geese, so as to use less fabric.

WHITE: 6⅜ yards (at least 41″ wide)

LIGHT PINK: 2¼ yards

HOT PINK: ¾ yard

PINK PRINT: 2 yards

BINDING: ⅞ yard

BACKING: 9 yards

BATTING: 108″ × 108″

CUTTING

WHITE
Cut 2 strips 10½″ × width of fabric; subcut into 2 squares 10½″ × 10½″ and 8 rectangles 10½″ × 5½″.

Cut 11 strips 5⅞″ × width of fabric; subcut into 64 squares 5⅞″ × 5⅞″.

Cut 9 strips 5½″ × width of fabric; subcut into 58 squares 5½″ × 5½″.

Cut 4 strips 20½″ × width of fabric; subcut into 3 rectangles 20½″ × 40½″ and 1 square 20½″ × 20½″.

TIP: It can be difficult to square up huge pieces of fabric, such as the white fabric needed for *Sweet Scarlet*. Instead, square up the yardage in sections. Measure about 1 yard of the fabric and adjust the layers so the selvages match. Square up the cut end, then cut the first few strips. Continue to measure out the next yard, trimming as needed to keep the edge square.

LIGHT PINK
Cut 7 strips 5⅞″ × width of fabric; subcut into 40 squares 5⅞″ × 5⅞″.

Cut 10 strips 3″ × width of fabric; subcut into 40 squares 3″ × 3″ and 40 rectangles 3″ × 5½″.

HOT PINK
Cut 7 strips 3″ × width of fabric; subcut into 80 squares 3″ × 3″.

PINK PRINT
Cut 4 strips 5⅞″ × width of fabric; subcut into 24 squares 5⅞″ × 5⅞″.

Cut 4 strips 10½″ × width of fabric; subcut into 8 squares 10½″ × 10½″ and 8 rectangles 10½″ × 5½″.

BINDING
Cut 11 strips 2½″ × width of fabric.

Designed and pieced by Lydia Nelson, quilted by Darlene Szabo

The corner block fabric is Pink Lucy Daisy by Liberty of London.

creation

Sew with right sides together and ¼″ seam allowances. Refer to Flying Geese (page 103) for extra guidance.

On all 64 white 5⅞″ × 5⅞″ squares, draw a line between diagonally opposite corners with a pencil.

Eight-Point Star Blocks

1. Sew together a light pink 3″ × 5½″ rectangle and 2 hot pink 3″ × 3″ squares to make a Flying Geese unit. Make 40. *figure A*

2. Assemble an Eight-Point Star by placing a white 5½″ × 5½″ square in the center, 4 Flying Geese on the sides, and 4 light pink 3″ × 3″ squares in the corners. Sew together the 3 columns and then sew together the block. Make 10. *figure B*

3. Make half-square triangles by pairing a white 5⅞″ × 5⅞″ square with a light pink 5⅞″ × 5⅞″ square, right sides together, and sewing ¼″ on either side of the pencil line. Cut apart on the line and press to make 2 half-square triangles. Make 80.

4. Sew together 2 of the units from Step 3 to make a Flying Geese unit. Make 40. *figure C*

5. Assemble a large Eight-Point Star by placing a smaller, completed Eight-Point Star block in the center, 4 Flying Geese units from Step 4 on the sides, and 4 white 5½″ × 5½″ squares in the corners. Sew together the 3 columns and then sew together the block. Make 10. *figure D*

A. Make 40.

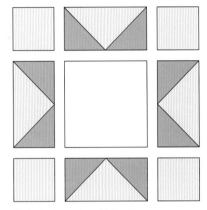

B. Eight-Point Star. Make 10.

C. Make 40.

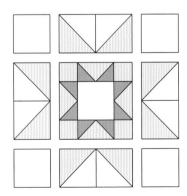

D. Large Eight-Point Star. Make 10.

corner blocks

1. Make half-square triangles by pairing a white 5⅞″ × 5⅞″ square with a pink print 5⅞″ × 5⅞″ square, right sides together, and sewing ¼″ on either side of the pencil line. Cut apart on the line and press to make 2 half-square triangles. Make 48.

E. Make 16.

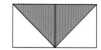

F. Make 8.

2. Sew together 32 half-square triangles with the white triangles in the center to make 16 Flying Geese. *figure E*

3. Sew the remaining 16 half-square triangles together with the pink print in the center to make 8 Flying Geese. *figure F*

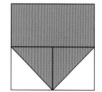

G. Make 8 Flying Geese squares.

4. Sew a pink print 5½″ × 10½″ rectangle to the pink print edge of a large Flying Geese unit from Step 3. Make 8 Flying Geese squares. *figure G*

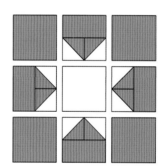

H. Make 2.

5. Assemble the block center by placing a white 10½″ × 10½″ square in the center, 4 large Flying Geese squares from Step 4 on the sides, and 4 pink print 10½″ × 10½″ squares in the corners. Sew together the 3 rows and then sew together the block. Make 2. *figure H*

6. Assemble the top and bottom strips by sewing together 2 large Flying Geese from Step 2 and then adding a white 5½″ × 5½″ square on each end. Make 4 and sew to the top and bottom of the 2 block centers from Step 5.

7. Assemble the side strips by sewing together 2 large Flying Geese from Step 2 and then adding a white 5½″ × 10½″ rectangle to each end. Make 4 and sew to the sides of the 2 block centers from Step 6. *figure I*

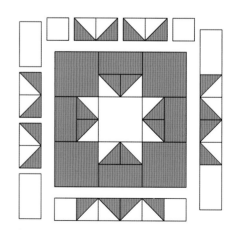

I. Corner block

quilt top assembly

1. Refer to the assembly diagram and sew 2 large Eight-Point Star blocks together. Make 4 pairs.

2. Sew a white 20½″ × 40½″ rectangle to a pair of large Eight-Point Star blocks. Make 2 units.

3. Sew a pair of large Eight-Point Star blocks to one side of the units from Step 2. Make 2 units.

4. Sew a corner block to the end of each unit from Step 3. Make 2.

5. Sew the white 20½″ × 20½″ square to the last white 20½″ × 40½″ rectangle. Then sew a large Eight-Point Star block to each end.

6. Sew each unit made in Step 4 to either side of the unit from Step 5. *figure J*

J. *Sweet Scarlet* assembly

quilting and binding

Refer to Quiltmaking Basics (pages 101–109) for instructions on backing, layering, basting, quilting, and double-fold straight-grain binding to finish *Sweet Scarlet*.

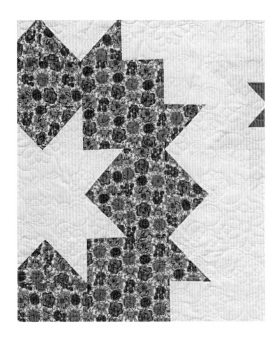

modern pioneer runner

Finished Block: 13″ × 16¼″ • **Finished Runner:** 16¾″ × 52½″

The fabrics for this runner are inspired by dreamy notions of earlier days, when fresh milk arrived to the table still warm and flour came in cotton sacks that were remade into dresses and quilts. It's a romanticized vision that comes to life today in the *Modern Pioneer Runner*. Don't be surprised if you have a craving for a small soirée after making this runner, even if it's just to show it off.

MATERIALS

Each block is a 13″ × 16¼″ rectangle. Decide how many blocks you need for the runner length you want. Materials and cutting instructions are presented per block for easy multiplying.

For each block:

RED PRINTS: ¼ yard total (a charm pack, mini charm pack, or scraps are good choices)

BLUE PRINT: ⅛ yard

WHITE: ⅜ yard

BINDING: ⅜ yard for up to 3 blocks; add 2½″ for each additional block

For runner:

BACKING: ½ yard for every 2 blocks

BATTING: ⅝ yard for up to 3 blocks

CUTTING

RED PRINTS
Cut 10 squares 2½″ × 2½″ and 8 squares 2⅛″ × 2⅛″.

BLUE PRINT
Cut 1 strip 2½″ × width of fabric; subcut into 8 squares 2½″ × 2½″.

Cut 1 strip 1½″ × width of fabric; subcut into 16 squares 1½″ × 1½″.

WHITE
Cut 1 strip 2½″ × width of fabric; subcut into 10 squares 2½″ × 2½″.

Cut 2 strips 2⅛″ × width of fabric; subcut into 8 squares 2⅛″ × 2⅛″ and 2 rectangles 2⅛″ × 13½″.

Cut 1 strip 1½″ × width of fabric; subcut into 16 squares 1½″ × 1½″.

Cut 1 strip 3¾″ × width of fabric; subcut into 2 squares 3¾″ × 3¾″ and 1 rectangle 3¾″ × 10¼″.

BINDING
Cut 4 strips 2½″ × width of fabric.

BACKING
Cut a piece 5″ longer and wider than the assembled blocks.

BATTING
Cut a piece 5″ longer and wider than the assembled blocks.

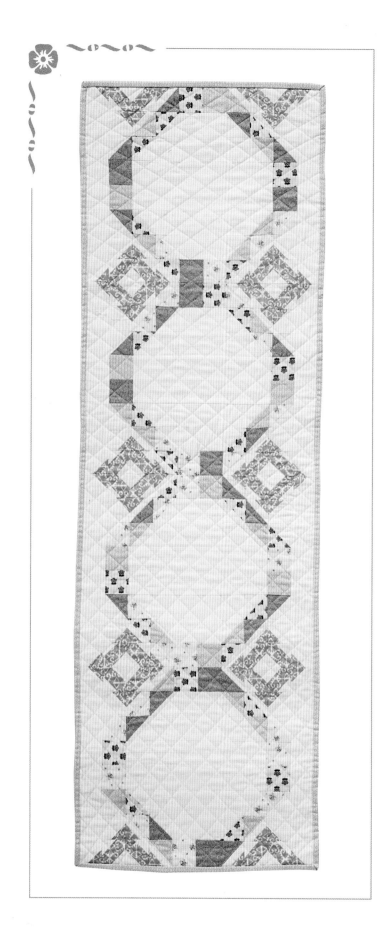

creation

Sew with right sides together and ¼˝ seam allowances. Refer to Sewing Diagonally (page 102) and Half-Square Triangles (page 102) for extra guidance.

1. Draw a line between diagonally opposite corners with a pencil on each white 2½˝ × 2½˝ square and on 8 blue 1½˝ × 1½˝ squares.

2. Pair a red 2½˝ × 2½˝ square and a white 2½˝ × 2½˝ square, right sides together, to make 2 half-square triangles. Make 20 per block. *figure A*

3. On 8 of the half-square triangles sew a blue 1½˝ × 1½˝ square to the corner of the white half as shown. Trim ¼˝ from the seamline and press open. Label these A. *figure B*

4. On 4 white 2⅛˝ × 2⅛˝ squares, sew a blue 1½˝ × 1½˝ square to a corner. Trim ¼˝ from the sewn line and press open. Label these B. *figure C*

5. On 8 blue 2½˝ × 2½˝ squares, sew 2 white 1½˝ × 1½˝ squares to opposite corners. Trim ¼˝ from the sewn line and press open. Label these C. *figure D*

6. On 2 white 2⅛˝ × 13½˝ rectangles, sew 2 blue 1½˝ × 1½˝ squares to the corners of a long edge. Trim and press open. *figure E*

7. Sew together 2 different red 2⅛˝ × 2⅛˝ squares. Trim and press open. Make 4 pairs. *figure F*

8. Sew a pair to each short side of a white 3¾˝ × 10¼˝ rectangle and label this D. *figure G*

A. Make 20 per block.

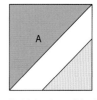

B. Make 8 per block.

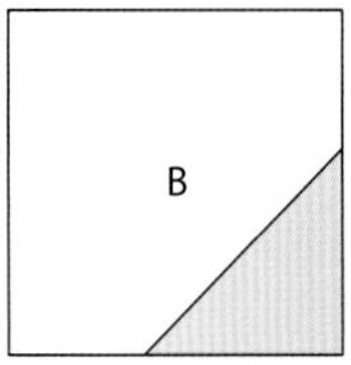

C. Make 4 per block.

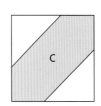

D. Make 8 per block.

E. Make 2 per block.

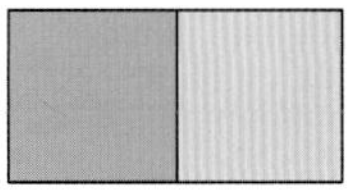

F. Make 4 pairs per block.

G. Make 1 per block.

9. Sew a pair to a white 3¾″ × 3¾″ square. Make 2 and label these E. *figure H*

10. Make 2 left corners. For row 1, sew together 2 half-square triangles and 1 white square 2⅛″ × 2⅛″. For row 2, sew together B, A, and a half-square triangle. For row 3, sew together 2 C units and 1 A. Join the rows. Make 2 per block. *figure I*

11. Make 2 right corners. For row 1, sew together a white 2⅛″ × 2⅛″ square and 2 half-square triangles. For row 2, sew together a half-square triangle, A, and B. For row 3, sew together A and 2 C units. Join the rows. Make 2 per block. *figure J*

12. Sew E between a left and a right corner. Make 2. *figure K*

H. Make 2 per block.

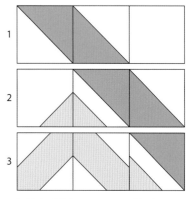

I. Make 2 left corners per block.

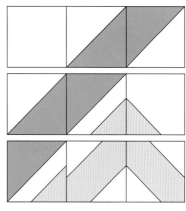

J. Make 2 right corners per block.

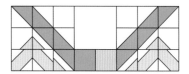

K. Make 2 per block.

13. Sew D between the units made in Step 12. *figure L*

14. Sew 2 long rectangles made in Step 6 to each side of the block and press open. *figure M*

quilting and binding

Refer to Quiltmaking Basics (pages 101–109) for instructions on backing, layering, basting, quilting, and double-fold straight-grain binding to finish your *Modern Pioneer Runner*.

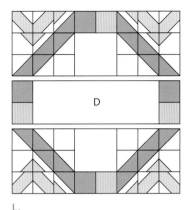

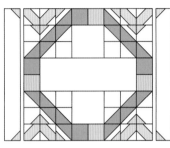

L.

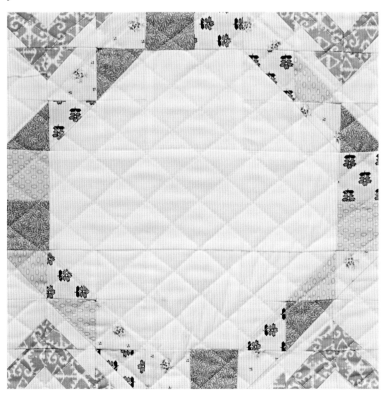

M.

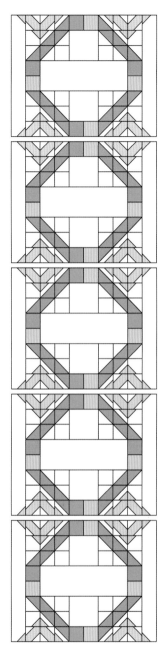

Runner layout

sampler pillow

Finished Block: 7″ × 7″ • Finished Pillow: 25″ × 25″

Pillows are an easy way to add a spot of color to a room. This *Sampler Pillow* also makes a great table topper—just omit the pillow form and pillow backing, then bind the edges.

MATERIALS

PINK: ¾ yard

PRINT: ½ yard

BLUE: ⅛ yard or fat eighth

QUILT BACKING: ⅞ yard

BATTING: 30″ × 30″

PILLOW BACKING: ¾ yard

PILLOW FORM: 24″ × 24″

TIP: With so many cut pieces, it's helpful to label each size with a sticky note to keep track!

CUTTING

PINK
Cut 1 strip 4⅜″ × width of fabric; subcut into 2 squares 4⅜″ × 4⅜″, 4 rectangles 2″ × 3¼″, and 8 rectangles 2¼″ × 4″.

Cut 1 strip 4″ × width of fabric; subcut into 5 squares 4″ × 4″, 2 squares 3⅝″ × 3⅝″, 2 squares 3⅛″ × 3⅛″, and 1 square 3″ × 3″.

Cut 1 strip 2¾″ × width of fabric; subcut into 1 square 2¾″ × 2¾″ and 10 squares 2⅝″ × 2⅝″.

Cut 1 strip 2½″ × width of fabric; subcut into 4 squares 2½″ × 2½″ and 8 squares 2¼″ × 2¼″.

Cut 1 strip 2″ × width of fabric; subcut into 8 squares 2″ × 2″.

Cut 6 strips 1½″ × width of fabric; piece strips as needed to subcut into 2 rectangles 1½″ × 25½″, 4 rectangles 1½″ × 23½″, and 6 rectangles 1½″ × 7½″.

PRINT
Cut 1 strip 3⅝″ × width of fabric; subcut into 2 squares 3⅝″ × 3⅝″, 2 squares 3⅛″ × 3⅛″, 8 squares 2¼″ × 2¼″, and 1 square 2″ × 2″.

Cut 1 strip 7½″ × width of fabric; subcut into 1 square 7½″ × 7½″, 8 rectangles 2¼″ × 4″, 2 squares 4⅜″ × 4⅜″, and 1 square 4″ × 4″.

Cut 1 strip 3″ × width of fabric; subcut into 2 rectangles 3″ × 5″ and 10 squares 2⅝″ × 2⅝″.

BLUE
Cut 1 strip 4″ × width of fabric; subcut into 4 rectangles 4″ × 2″ and 4 rectangles 2½″ × 2″.

QUILT BACKING
Cut 1 square 30″ × 30″.

PILLOW BACKING
Cut 2 pieces 15″ × 25½″.

Photo by Lydia Nelson

The print fabric is Sophie by Chez Moi for Moda.

creation

Sew with right sides together and ¼″ seam allowances. Refer to Half-Square Triangles (page 102) and Flying Geese (page 103) for extra guidance.

Block 1

1. Pair a pink 4⅜″ × 4⅜″ square and a print 4⅜″ × 4⅜″ square, right sides together, to make 2 half-square triangles. Make 4. *figure A*

2. Piece together the half-square triangles to complete the block. *figure B*

Block 2

1. Pair a pink 3⅛″ × 3⅛″ square and a print 3⅛″ × 3⅛″ square, right sides together, to make 2 half-square triangles. Make 4. *You will only use 3 of these.*

2. Sew together 3 half-square triangles and a pink 2¾″ × 2¾″ square. Sew a print 3″ × 5″ rectangle to the bottom. Sew a pink 3″ × 3″ square to a short side of a second print 3″ × 5″ rectangle and sew this new piece to the right side of the block to complete the block. *figure C*

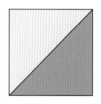

A. Half-square triangle

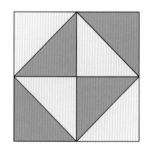

B. Block 1

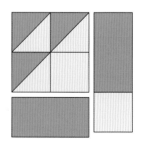

C. Block 2

Block 3

1. Pair a pink 2⅝″ × 2⅝″ square and a print 2⅝″ × 2⅝″ square, right sides together, to make 2 half-square triangles. Make 4.

2. Draw a diagonal line on the wrong side of 4 pink 2¼″ × 2¼″ squares. Sew each to the top right corners of the print 2¼″ × 4″ rectangles. Press and trim. Make 4.

3. Sew 2 of the half-square triangles made in Step 1 to the top and bottom of a rectangle made in Step 2. Note the orientation of the half-square triangles. Make 2.

4. Sew the remaining 2 rectangles to the top and bottom of a pink 4″ × 4″ square as shown.

5. Sew together 3 columns to complete the block. *figure D*

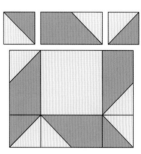

D. Block 3

Block 4

Sew together a pink 2¼″ × 4″ rectangle and a print 2¼″ × 4″ rectangle along their long edges, forming a square. Make 4 and sew them together to complete the block. *figure E*

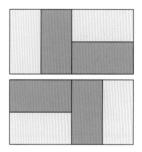

E. Block 4

Block 5

1. Draw a diagonal line on the wrong side of 8 pink 2″ × 2″ squares. Sew a pink square to the top right corner of a blue 2″ × 2½″ rectangle. Press and trim. Make 4. Sew a pink 2½″ × 2½″ square to the left side of each unit. *figure F*

F.   G.

2. Sew a pink 2″ × 2″ square to the top right corner of a blue 2″ × 4″ rectangle. Press and trim. Make 4. *figure G*

3. Sew together the rectangles made in Steps 1 and 2 and then sew those 4 units together to complete the block. *figure H*

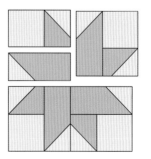

H. Block 5

Block 6

1. Pair a pink 3⅝″ × 3⅝″ square and a print 3⅝″ × 3⅝″ square, right sides together, to make 2 half-square triangles. Make 4.

2. Sew a pink 2″ × 3¼″ rectangle between each pair of 2 half-square triangles from Step 1. Make 2.

3. Sew a print 2″ × 2″ square between 2 pink 2″ × 3¼″ rectangles.

4. Sew together all 3 pieces to complete the block. *figure I*

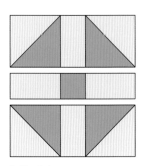

I. Block 6

Block 7

Sew 2 pink 4″ × 4″ squares to opposite corners of a print 7½″ × 7½″ square. Press open and repeat on the remaining corners. *figure J*

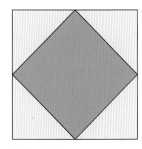

J. Block 7

Block 8

1. Draw a diagonal line on the wrong side of 8 pink 2⅝″ × 2⅝″ squares. Place the pink 2⅝″ × 2⅝″ square on top of a print 2⅝″ × 2⅝″ square, right sides together, and sew ¼″ on either side of the pencil line. Cut apart on the pencil line and press to make 2 half-square triangles. Make 16.

2. Sew together 4 half-square triangles to form a row. Sew together the rows as shown to complete the block. *figure K*

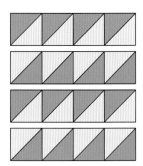

K. Block 8

Block 9

1. Draw a diagonal line on the wrong side of 2 print 2¼″ × 2¼″ squares and sew them to the corners of a pink 2¼″ × 4″ rectangle to make a Flying Geese unit. Repeat to make 4.

2. Sew pink 2¼″ × 2¼″ squares to each end of 2 Flying Geese. Sew a print 4″ × 4″ square between the remaining 2 Flying Geese. Sew together the 3 strips to complete the block. *figure L*

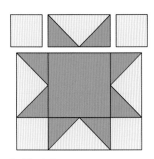

L. Block 9

pillow top assembly

1. Arrange the completed blocks in 3 rows of 3.

2. Add the 6 rectangles of 1½˝ × 7½˝ sashing between the blocks in each row.

3. Add the 4 rectangles of 1½˝ × 23½˝ sashing between the rows and at the top and bottom.

4. Add the 2 rectangles of 1½˝ × 25½˝ sashing to the sides.

5. Sew the rows together to complete the top. *figure M*

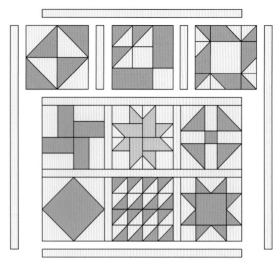

M. Pillow top layout

pillow assembly

1. Treat the pillow top as a small quilt. Refer to Quiltmaking Basics (pages 101–109) for instructions on backing, layering, basting, and quilting.

2. On each of the 2 backing pieces, press under a long edge ¼˝. Press under ¼˝ once more to hide the raw seam, and stitch down this hem.

3. Match the pillow top and backing pieces with right sides together. The finished edges of the backing will overlap near the center back. Sew around the perimeter of the pillow with a ¼˝ seam, backstitching at the beginning and end. Trim the corners, turn the cover right side out, and insert a pillow form. *figure N*

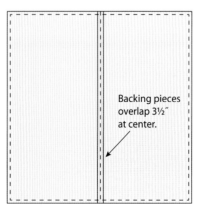

Backing pieces overlap 3½˝ at center.

N. Assemble pillow cover.

evergreen pillow

Finished Block: 4″ × 4″ • **Finished Pillow Top:** 18″ × 18″

The *Evergreen Pillow* makes a striking design statement any time of year. Its two-tone design is bold enough to stand alone, but a small forest of these trees on a sofa would look elegant and festive around Christmastime. For a dreamy look, choose a subdued green.

MATERIALS

GREEN: ¼ yard

WHITE: ⅝ yard

BROWN: 1 piece 2½″ × 3½″ for tree trunk

QUILT BACKING: ¾ yard

BATTING: 23″ × 23″

PILLOW BACKING: ⅜ yard

PILLOW FORM: 18″ × 18″

CUTTING

GREEN
Cut 2 strips 2½″ × width of fabric; subcut into 20 squares 2½″ × 2½″.

Cut 1 strip 1¼″ × width of fabric; subcut into 10 squares 1¼″ × 1¼″.

WHITE
Cut 2 strips 2½″ × width of fabric; subcut into 20 squares 2½″ × 2½″ and 2 rectangles 2½″ × 8″.

Cut 2 strips 2⅛″ × width of fabric; subcut into 40 rectangles 2⅛″ × 1¼″.

Cut 1 strip 4½″ × width of fabric; subcut into 2 rectangles 4½″ × 2½″, 2 squares 4½″ × 4½″, and 2 rectangles 4½″ × 6½″.

Cut 1 strip 1½″ × width of fabric; subcut into 2 rectangles 1½″ × 18½″.

QUILT BACKING
Cut 1 square 23 × 23″.

PILLOW BACKING
Cut 2 rectangles 11½″ × 18½″.

creation

Sew with right sides together and ¼˝ seam allowances. Refer to Half-Square Triangles (page 102) for extra guidance.

1. Pair a white 2½˝ × 2½˝ square and a green 2½˝ × 2½˝ square, right sides together, to make 2 half-square triangles. Make 40. *figure A*

2. Sew a white 1¼˝ × 2⅛˝ rectangle between 2 half-square triangles. Make 20. *figure B*

3. Sew a green 1¼˝ × 1¼˝ square between 2 white 1¼˝ × 2⅛˝ rectangles. Make 10. *figure C*

4. Sew together the strips made in Steps 2 and 3 to complete a block. Make 10. *figure D*

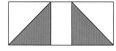

A. Make 40.

B. Make 20.

C. Make 10.

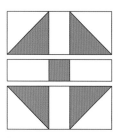

D. Tree block

pillow top assembly

1. Sew together 4 tree blocks.

2. Sew together 3 tree blocks and sew a white 2½″ × 4½″ rectangle to each end.

3. Sew together 2 tree blocks and sew a white 4½″ × 4½″ square to each end.

4. Sew a white 4½″ × 6½″ rectangle to each end of the remaining tree block.

5. Sew a white 2½″ × 8″ rectangle to each end of the 2½″ × 3″ tree trunk piece.

6. Sew together all the rows and sew 2 strips 1½″ × 18½″ to the sides. *figure E*

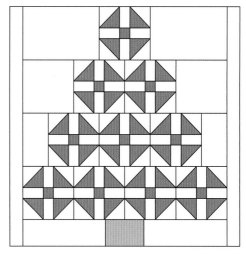

E. *Evergreen Pillow* assembly

pillow assembly

Refer to the Pillow Assembly (page 85) instructions that are included with the *Sampler Pillow* project for directions on finishing the quilted pillow top, making the backing, and completing the cover.

bloom pillow

Finished Pillow: 18″ × 18″

Want a break from piecing? Here's a design that's all about appliqué. The *Bloom Pillow* features floral shapes that bring nature inside to give a home panache. And the small pattern pieces mean you can cull from your stash to create colorful flowers that fit your taste and home styling.

MATERIALS

WHITE: ⅝ yard

FLORAL: ¼ yard

GREEN: ⅛ yard

PINK: 3 squares 2″ × 2″

LIGHT FUSIBLE WEB: ½ yard

QUILT BACKING: ¾ yard

BATTING: 23″ × 23″

PILLOW BACKING: ⅜ yard

PILLOW FORM: 18″ × 18″

CUTTING

WHITE
Cut 1 square 18½″ × 18½″.

QUILT BACKING
Cut 1 square 23″ × 23″.

PILLOW BACKING
Cut 2 rectangles 11½″ × 18½″.

creation

Appliqué

Use the *Bloom Pillow* pattern pieces and follow the instructions in Appliqué (page 93) to add the flower, leaf, and circle shapes to the pillow top. Refer to the appliqué assembly diagram for guidance on where to place the pieces. *figure A*

pillow assembly

Refer to the Pillow Assembly (page 85) instructions that are included with the *Sampler Pillow* project for directions on finishing the quilted pillow top, making the backing, and completing the cover.

A. Appliqué assembly

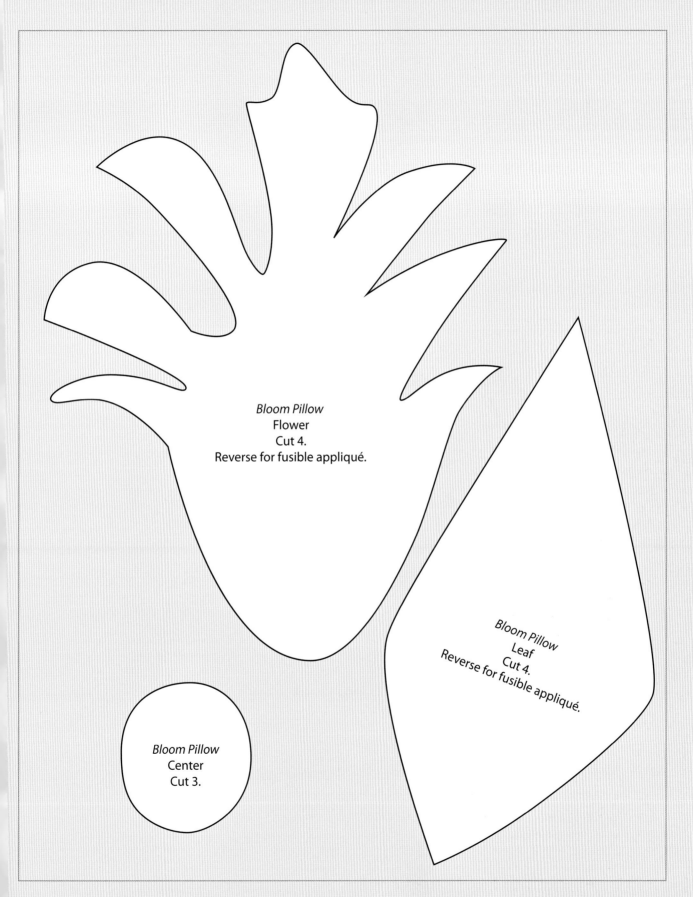

Bloom Pillow
Flower
Cut 4.
Reverse for fusible appliqué.

Bloom Pillow
Leaf
Cut 4.
Reverse for fusible appliqué.

Bloom Pillow
Center
Cut 3.

woof!
a dog bed

Finished Block: 15″ × 15″ • **Finished Bed:** 44″ round or 45″ × 45″ square

We dog owners love our pooches, despite their sloppy habits. Here's a quilted dog bed that relies on a durable painter's drop cloth for rugged sensibility. Plus, its shabby-chic charm makes for a happy owner. Make *Woof!* square or round to suit your style.

MATERIALS

Square dog beds are tough to find and can be pricey. An inexpensive twin-size comforter works well too and can be purchased easily at IKEA or Target. Just fold the comforter to fit. Another plus? A comforter can be thrown in the washing machine!

BLUE FLORAL: ⅜ yard

BLUE STRIPE: ¾ yard

LIGHT BLUE: ¼ yard

PAINTER'S DROP CLOTH: 6′ × 9′

BATTING: 53″ × 53″

BACKING: 2 yards muslin or other fabric

DOG BED INSERT: 44″ round or 45″ square

CUTTING

BLUE FLORAL

Cut 1 strip 4⅝″ × width of fabric; subcut into 6 squares 4⅝″ × 4⅝″.

Cut 1 strip 3⅛″ × width of fabric; subcut into 8 squares 3⅛″ × 3⅛″.

BLUE STRIPE

Cut 2 strips 6⅛″ × width of fabric; subcut into 8 squares 6⅛″ × 6⅛″; cut each square once diagonally. Label these *Triangle A*.

Cut 1 strip 4⅝″ × width of fabric; subcut into 4 squares 4⅝″ × 4⅝″.

Cut 2 strips 3½″ × width of fabric; subcut into 16 squares 3½″ × 3½″.

Cut 2 strips 3⅛″ × width of fabric; subcut into 16 squares 3⅛″ × 3⅛″.

CUTTING continued on page 96

Pieced and designed by Lydia Nelson, quilted by Darlene Szabo

LIGHT BLUE

Cut 1 strip 4⅝″ × width of fabric; subcut into 6 squares 4⅝″ × 4⅝″.

PAINTER'S DROP CLOTH

FOR ROUND BED: Cut 2 strips 5½″ × 71″ for gusset

FOR SQUARE BED: Cut 3 strips 5½″ × 61″ for gusset

FOR EITHER BED: Cut 1 rectangle 36″ × 60″; subcut into 2 strips 15½″ × 60″.

From each of these strips, subcut 2 squares 15½″ × 15½″.

From the remaining 15½″ × 29″ pieces:

Cut 2 strips 6⅛″ × 29″; subcut into 8 squares 6⅛″ × 6⅛″ and cut the squares once diagonally. Label these *Triangle A*.

Cut 2 strips 3½″ × 29″; subcut into 16 squares 3½″ × 3½″.

Cut 1 strip 3⅛″ × 29″; subcut into 8 squares 3⅛″ × 3⅛″.

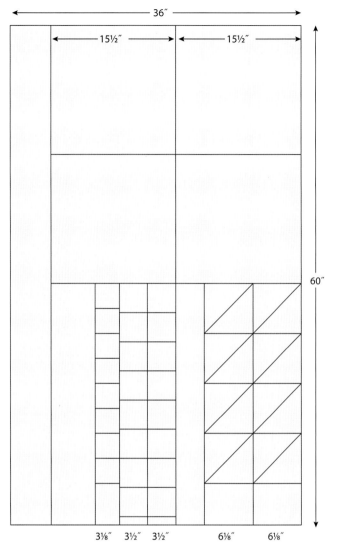

Cutting layout

creation

Sew with right sides together and ¼″ seam allowances except where indicated for the appliqué. Refer to Sewing Diagonally (page 102) and Half-Square Triangles (page 102) for extra guidance.

The 4 outside blocks are each composed of 4 pieced right triangles, in 2 different styles. I will refer to the 2 styles as Triangle 1 and Triangle 2.

Half-Square Triangles

Pair a blue stripe 3½″ × 3½″ square with a drop cloth 3½″ × 3½″ square to make 2 half-square triangles. Make 32. *figure A*

A. Make 32.

Triangle 1

1. Sew a blue stripe 3⅛″ × 3⅛″ square to a half-square triangle along the blue side, forming a rectangle, as shown in the top row of Figure B. Make 8.

2. Sew a blue stripe 3⅛″ × 3⅛″ square to a half-square triangle along the drop cloth side, forming a rectangle, as shown in the bottom row of Figure B. Make 8.

B. Make 8.

3. Sew together 1 of each rectangle from Steps 1 and 2 to form a square. Make 8. *figure B*

4. Sew a drop cloth Triangle A to a square along the blue stripe side. Press the seams toward Triangle A. Repeat on the other side to make Triangle 1. Make 8. *figure C*

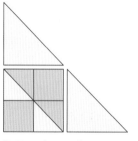

C. Triangle 1. Make 8.

Triangle 2

1. Sew a drop cloth 3⅛″ × 3⅛″ square to a half-square triangle along the drop cloth side to make a rectangle, as shown in the top row of Figure D. Make 8.

2. Sew a blue floral 3⅛″ × 3⅛″ square to a half-square triangle along the blue stripe side to make a rectangle, as shown in the bottom row of Figure D. Make 8.

D. Make 8.

3. Sew together 1 of each rectangle from Steps 1 and 2 to form a square. *figure D*

4. Sew a blue stripe Triangle A to a square along the drop cloth side. Press the seams toward Triangle A. Repeat on the other side to make Triangle 2. Make 8. *figure E*

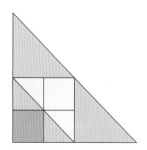

E. Triangle 2. Make 8.

Block 1

Sew Triangle 1 to Triangle 2 to make a large right triangle. Make 8. Sew together 2 large right triangles, forming Block 1. Make 4. *figure F*

Block 2

1. Pair a light blue $4\frac{5}{8}'' \times 4\frac{5}{8}''$ square with a blue stripe $4\frac{5}{8}'' \times 4\frac{5}{8}''$ square to make 2 half-square triangles. Make 4. *figure G*

2. Pair a light blue $4\frac{5}{8}'' \times 4\frac{5}{8}''$ square with a blue floral $4\frac{5}{8}'' \times 4\frac{5}{8}''$ square to make 2 half-square triangles. Make 8. *figure H*

3. Pair a blue stripe $4\frac{5}{8}'' \times 4\frac{5}{8}''$ square with a blue floral $4\frac{5}{8}'' \times 4\frac{5}{8}''$ square to make 2 half-square triangles. Make 4. *figure I*

4. Assemble the squares as shown. Sew together strips of 4 half-square triangles to form 4 rows. Sew together the rows to make Block 2. *figure J*

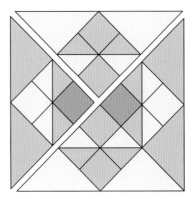

F. Block 1. Make 4.

G. Make 4.

H. Make 4.

I. Make 4.

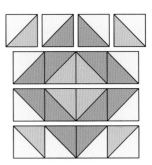

J. Block 2. Make 1.

quilt top assembly

Lay out 4 Block 1 squares, a Block 2 square, and 4 drop cloth 15½″ × 15½″ squares. Sew together the 3 rows and then sew the rows together to make the quilt top. *figure K*

quilting and finishing

Add backing and batting to the quilt top and quilt as desired. Refer to Quiltmaking Basics (pages 101–109) for instructions on backing, layering, basting, and quilting.

For a Round Dog Bed

1. Lay the quilt on a flat, clean surface. Construct a large compass by safety pinning a 25″ piece of string to the exact center of the finished quilt top. Tie a pencil to the string so that the pencil tip is 22¼″ from the center when the pencil is held perpendicular to the quilt top. Keeping the string taut, hold the pencil straight up and down and slowly trace a circle around the quilt top. Cut along the pencil line. *figure L*

2. From the painter's drop cloth, cut 2 semicircle pieces from the backing fabric. Use the 44½″ round quilt top, folded in half, as a pattern but add an extra 3½″ to the folded edge. Press each flat edge under ½″ twice and stitch the hem. *figure M*

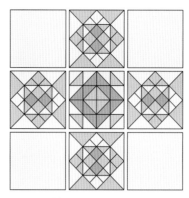

K. Assembly

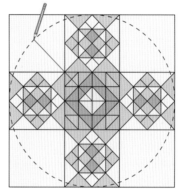

L. Use makeshift compass to draw circle on quilt top.

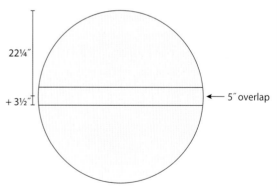

22¼″

+ 3½″ ← 5″ overlap

M. Quilt top layout and backing

3. Sew the gusset pieces end to end along 5½″ sides and trim to 5½″ × 138¾″. Sew together to form a large circle. Pin around the quilt top and sew with a ¼″ seam. Sew over once more to secure.

4. With the flat edges facing the center and both pieces right side up, position the backing pieces together so they form a 44½″ circle. They will overlap 5″. Pin or baste the overlapped edges together.

5. Place the gusset (now joined with the quilt top) on top of the backing pieces, right sides together, and pin evenly around the backing. Sew with a ¼″ seam. Sew around once more to secure. The dog bed will be inside out at this point.

6. Turn the bed right side out and insert the bed form or folded comforter.

For a Square Dog Bed

1. From the painter's drop cloth, cut 2 pieces of backing 25″ × 45½″. On each backing piece, fold over a 25″ edge ½″ and press. Fold over ½″ once more and stitch the hem.

2. Sew the gusset pieces end to end along 5½″ sides and trim to 5½″ × 180½″. Stitch together end to end along 5½″ sides to form a large circle. Pin around the quilt top and sew with a ¼″ seam. As you sew around each corner, round the quilt top corner slightly. Sew over the stitching once more to secure.

3. With the finished edges facing the center and both pieces right side up, position the backing pieces so they form a 45½″ × 45½″ square. They will overlap 5″. Pin or baste the overlapped edges together. Refer to Steps 5 and 6 (above) of the round dog bed instructions for directions on finishing.

quiltmaking basics

general guidelines

Seam Allowances

All the seams in this book are ¼˝ unless otherwise noted. Use a ¼˝ presser foot, seam gauge, tape on the machine's throat plate, or another method for accuracy.

To avoid frustration, test your ¼˝ seam before starting a project. Cut 2 fabric scraps into 2˝ × 2˝ squares and sew them together along a side, aligning the raw edges. Open up the fabric, press the seam open, and measure across. If the rectangle doesn't measure *exactly* 3½˝ across, you will need to tweak your method or the quilt blocks won't fit together.

Piecing

There is no need to backstitch when piecing, unless otherwise noted. Usually seamlines are crossed by other seams, and that stitching anchors them.

Pinning

I hate pinning fabric. There, I said it! But we all need to take the time to pin every few inches and at every seam intersection. Many times

I have overestimated my ability to just hold together fabric pieces and feed them into the machine, only to end up with wonky seams.

Pressing

In general, press seams toward the darker fabric. Press lightly in an up-and-down motion. Avoid using a very hot iron or moving the iron back and forth, which can distort the shapes and blocks. Be especially careful when pressing bias edges, as they stretch easily.

When joining pieces with seams that meet, make sure the allowances are pressed in opposite directions. They should nestle together so that the fabric pieces lock together, stay aligned, and are less bulky.

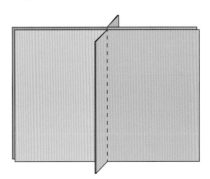

Nested seams

Sewing Diagonally

When you need to sew a square along its diagonal, there is no raw edge to line up with the edge of the presser foot. The most accurate approach is to draw a stitching line right on the fabric. But when you have scores of such pieces, it can be time-consuming to mark each one.

Here are three techniques to try:

1. Mark a stitching line on your sewing surface by placing a strip of low-tack painter's tape on the machine bed. The right edge of the tape should be aligned with the point of the needle. Place the corners of the square directly on top of the tape edge.

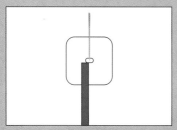 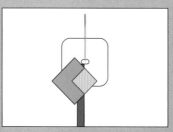

Sewing diagonally using tape as guide

2. The fast2sew Ultimate Seam Guide is a tool designed just for this task. Simply align the points of the square with the center line as you would with tape.

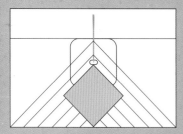

3. With squares so large they hang beyond the edge of your seam guide or tape, use a pencil and ruler to draw a line between opposite corners on the wrong side of the fabric and sew on top of this line.

half-square triangles

Refer to the project instructions for the size of the squares.

1. With right sides together, pair 2 squares. Draw a diagonal line from corner to corner on the wrong side of the top square.

Draw line.

2. Sew 2 rows of stitching a scant ¼˝ on either side of the drawn line.

Sew.

3. Cut on the drawn line.

4. Press toward the darker fabric and trim away the dog-ears, if desired.

Half-square triangle

flying geese

Refer to the project instructions for the sizes of the squares and rectangle.

1. A Flying Geese block is made by sewing 2 squares along their diagonals to the opposite sides of a rectangle. Draw a diagonal line from corner to corner on the wrong sides of the 2 squares. *figure A*

A. Draw diagonal line.

2. With right sides together, place a square on an end of the rectangle. Sew directly on the drawn line and trim the seam allowance to ¼″. *figure B*

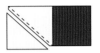

B. Sew on drawn line and trim.

3. Flip back the remaining triangle and press the seam open. Trim away the dog-ears, if desired. *figure C*

C.

4. Repeat Steps 1–3 on the other side. With right sides together, place the remaining square on the other end of the rectangle. Sew directly on the line, trim the seam allowance to ¼″, and press open. *figures D & E*

D. Sew on drawn line and trim.

TIP: Two half-square triangles can be sewn together to make a Flying Geese block that has a seam down the middle. I prefer this method when making large Flying Geese, as there is less waste than with the traditional method, in which the entire other halves of the squares are trimmed off and discarded.

E. Flying Geese block

appliqué

1. Trace the reverse or mirror image of all the parts of an appliqué shape onto the paper side of fusible web. Write the pattern letter or number on each traced shape.

2. Cut around the appliqué shapes, leaving a ¼″ margin around each piece.

3. Iron each fusible web shape to the wrong side of the appropriate fabric, following the manufacturer's instructions for fusing. I don't worry about the grainline when placing the

pieces. Cut on top of the traced lines and peel off the paper backing. A thin layer of fusible web will remain on the wrong side of the fabric.

4. Position the pieces where directed. Press to fuse them in place.

5. Machine stitch around the appliqué pieces using a zigzag, satin, or blanket stitch. The type of stitching you use and the thread color you select are personal aesthetic choices.

borders and sashing

Strips are cut the width of the fabric. Piece them together to achieve the needed lengths. I prefer butted borders; however, I've included mitered corner border instructions, if you'd like to give them a try.

Butted Borders

In most cases the side borders are sewn on first.

1. Measure the length of the quilt top through the center. This will be the length to cut the side borders. Piece strips to this length if needed. *figure A*

2. Pin the side borders to the quilt top first, matching the centers and ends of each side of the quilt top to the center and ends of each side border. Using a ¼″ seam allowance, sew the borders to the quilt top and press the seams toward the border. *figure B*

3. Measure the width of the quilt top through the center, including the side borders. This will be the length to cut or piece the top and bottom borders. Repeat Step 2 to add these borders. *figures C & D*

A.

B.

C.

D.

Mitered Corner Borders

1. Measure the length of the quilt top and add 2 times the cut width of the border, plus 5″. This is the length you need to cut or piece the side borders.

2. Pin the side borders to the quilt top, matching the centers.

3. Using a ¼″ seam allowance, sew the borders to the quilt top, starting and stopping ¼″ from the top and bottom quilt top edges and backstitching at each end. The excess length of the side borders will extend beyond the edges. Press the seams toward the borders. *figure F*

Start stitching ¼″ from edge of quilt top.

F. Stitching border to quilt

4. Determine the length needed for the top and bottom border in the same way, measuring the width of the quilt top through the center, including the side borders. Add 2 times the cut width of the border plus 5″ to this measurement. Cut or piece the top and bottom border strips to this length.

5. Repeat Steps 2 and 3 to add the top and bottom borders to the quilt top.

6. To create the miter, lay the corner on the ironing board. Working with the quilt right side up, lay a border strip on top of the adjacent border. *figure G*

7. With right sides up, fold the top border strip under itself so that it meets the edge of the adjacent border and forms a 45° angle. Pin the fold in place. *figure H*

8. Position a 90°-angle triangle or ruler over the corner to check that the corner is flat and square. When everything is in place, press the fold firmly. *figure I*

9. Remove the pins. Fold the center section of the top diagonally from the corner, right sides together, and align the long edges of the border strips. On the wrong side, place pins near the pressed fold in the corner to secure the border strips.

10. Begin sewing at the inside corner and backstitch to secure. Stitch along the fold toward the outside point of the border corner, being careful not to allow any stretching to occur. Backstitch at the end. Trim the excess border fabric to a ¼″ seam allowance. Press the seam open. *figure J*

G. Place border strips on top of each other at quilt corners.

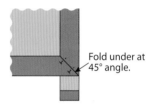

Fold under at 45° angle.

H. Fold border strip.

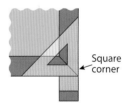

Square corner

I. Use right angle or gridded ruler to check that corner is square.

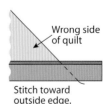

Wrong side of quilt

Stitch toward outside edge.

J. Stitch mitered corner along fold.

backing

For quilts, cut the backing at least 8″ longer and wider than the quilt top. Piece the backing if necessary. Trim away the selvages before piecing the backing. For smaller, pillow-size quilts, the backing needs to be only about 4″ longer and wider than the quilt top.

batting

There are many choices when it comes to batting. Consult your local quilt shop to learn about the different materials and thicknesses available. I use 100% cotton batting, but wool batting is a good option for chillier areas. Note that your batting choice may have an effect on the quilting design. Check the manufacturer's instructions to see how far apart the quilting lines can be. Cut the batting approximately 8″ longer and wider than the quilt top. For pillow-size quilts, cut the batting 4″ longer and wider than the quilt.

layering

Spread the backing wrong side up on a table or the floor and tape down the edges with masking tape. (When working on carpet, secure the backing to the carpet with T-pins.) Center the batting on top of the backing and smooth out any folds. Place the quilt top right side up on top of the batting and backing, making sure it is centered.

basting

Basting keeps the backing, batting, and quilt top—the quilt "sandwich" layers—from shifting while you are quilting. I highly recommend quilt basting spray and curved basting safety pins.

For machine quilting, pin baste the quilt layers together with safety pins placed about 3″–4″ apart. Begin pin basting in the center and move toward the edges, first in vertical, then horizontal, rows. Try not to pin directly on intended quilting lines.

For hand quilting, baste the layers together by hand, stitching with a long needle and light-colored thread. Knot one end of the thread. Use long stitches. Begin in the center and move out toward the edges in vertical and horizontal rows approximately 4″ apart. Add two diagonal rows of basting.

quilting

Quilting, whether by hand or machine, has both an aesthetic role and a functional role. You may choose to quilt in-the-ditch, echo the pieced or appliqué motifs, use patterns from quilting design books and stencils, or do free-motion quilting. Remember to check the batting manufacturer's recommendations for how close together the quilting lines must be.

Another option is to hire a professional to do the quilting. Ask for recommendations at your local fabric store or see the Resources section.

trim detailing

Adding trim to a quilt at the bound edge is a great way to add detail. Sew trim around the perimeter of a quilt top just over the ¼″ binding seamline, before sewing on the binding. Fold trim over the binding, and press. As long as the trim is wider than ¼″, it will stick out beyond the binding and give the quilt extra dimension. Trims such as rickrack or lace can also be used for a classic, vintage look. *figures K & L*

K. Stitch trim ¼″ from edge.

L. Press trim over binding.

binding

Before adding binding to the edge of a quilt, trim the excess batting and backing ¼″ beyond the seamline to give the binding some thickness and stability.

Double-Fold Straight-Grain Binding

1. For a ¼″ finished binding, cut strips 2½″ wide and piece them together with diagonal seams to make a continuous binding strip. Trim the seam allowances to ¼″. Press the seams open. *figures M & N*

2. Press the entire strip in half lengthwise with wrong sides together. With raw edges even, pin the binding to the front edge of the quilt, starting a few inches away from a corner and leaving the first few inches of the binding unattached. Sew the binding through all the quilt layers, using a ¼″ seam allowance and a walking foot if you have one.

Stop ¼″ away from the first corner and backstitch a stitch. *figure O*

TIP: A walking foot grips the top fabric in unison with the feed dogs below, making it very useful for keeping multiple layers from shifting.

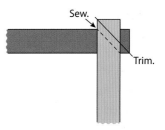

M. Sew together binding strips using diagonal seams to reduce bulk.

N. Completed diagonal seam in binding strip

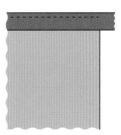

O. End stitching ¼″ from corner.

3. Lift the presser foot and needle. Rotate the quilt a quarter-turn. Fold the binding at a right angle so it extends straight above the quilt and the fold forms a 45° angle in the corner. *figure P*

4. Fold down the binding strip so that the fold is even with the top edge of the quilt and the raw edges are even on the right side. *figure Q*

5. Begin sewing at the top of the folded edge. Repeat in the same manner at all the corners. Continue stitching until you are back near the beginning of the binding strip. See Finishing the Binding Ends (page 109) for tips on how to finish and hide the raw edges of the ends of the binding.

Continuous Bias Binding

Bias-cut binding has more stretch than straight-grain binding and is useful for binding scalloped edges and other curves. An easy way to make bias binding is by first sewing a tube of fabric and then cutting a continuous strip from it.

1. Start with a square of fabric and cut it apart into 2 right triangles. With right sides facing, place one triangle on top of the other so that a short edge of each triangle lines up but the remaining points do not. Sew together the triangles along the aligned short edges using a ¼˝ seam allowance. Press the seam open. *figure R*

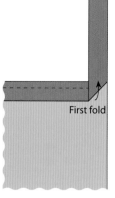

P. Fold up binding to form 45° angle in corner.

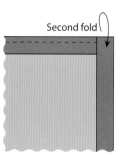

Q. Fold down binding strip, keeping fold and raw edges aligned.

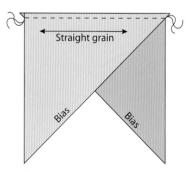

R. Sew together triangles, matching 2 short edges.

2. Using a ruler, mark the parallelogram created by the 2 triangles with lines spaced apart the width needed for the binding strips. Cut about 5˝ along the first line. *figure S*

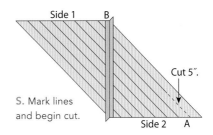

S. Mark lines and begin cut.

3. The next step is to join together Side 1 and Side 2, forming a tube. The raw edge at point A will align with the raw edge at B. The first line will be offset by a strip width. Pin together the raw edges with right sides facing, making sure that the drawn lines match. *figure T*

4. Sew with a ¼˝ seam allowance. Press open the seam. Cut along the drawn lines with scissors, creating a continuous strip.

5. Press the entire strip in half lengthwise with wrong sides facing. Attach the binding to the quilt as described in Double-Fold Straight-Grain Binding (page 107).

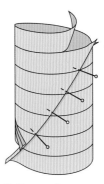

T. Pin together so cut strip is free and all lines match.

Finishing the Binding Ends

This is the way I like to finish my binding ends.

1. Leave about 5˝ of binding unsewn at the beginning. After stitching around the quilt, fold back the ending tail of the binding on itself at the point where it meets the beginning of the binding. Press with a hot iron. From that fold, measure and make a mark ½˝ from the fold. Trim the tail along the mark. *figure U*

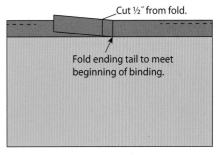

U. Trim binding tail to same length as width of binding.

2. Unfold both binding ends and place right sides together, then sew together with a ¼˝ seam. Press open.

3. Refold the binding and stitch the unattached portion to the quilt, backstitching at the beginning and end. Fold over the raw edges of the binding to the quilt back and hand stitch. Use the machine-stitched line as a guide to keep the binding even.

resources

Quilting Services:

Kathy Olkowski provides mail-in quilting services. Find out more at kathystitchbystitch.blogspot.com.

Melanie Simpson owns Front Porch Quilt Shoppe, in Ozark, Alabama, and provides mail-in quilting services. Visit her website at frontporchquiltshoppe.com.

Darlene Szabo and Debby Bond own Sew Graceful Quilting in Rogers, Arkansas, and provide mail-in quilting services. Visit their website at sewgracefulquilting.com.

Supplies:

The 44˝ dog bed insert was purchased from L.L.Bean (llbean.com).

The fast2sew Ultimate Seam Guide from C&T Publishing can be found at your local quilt shop or ctpub.com.

Helpful Books:

Beginner's Guide to Free-Motion Quilting by Natalia Bonner

First Steps to Free-Motion Quilting by Christina Cameli

The Practical Guide to Patchwork by Elizabeth Hartman

about the author

Lydia Nelson was born in Detroit, Michigan, and grew up in Dearborn and Saline, Michigan. She graduated from Purdue University with a degree in management.

Her love of fiber arts runs deep and includes studying apparel design and knitting samples for her mom's yarn shop, Mockingbird Moon, in Rogers, Arkansas. Lydia resides in Saline, Michigan, with her husband and three boys, and she enjoys hot yoga, cycling, and high-intensity Tabata training to counteract all the brownies, chocolate milk, and Oreos she consumes.

You can read her blog at lydianelson.typepad.com.

Photo by Wade Canfield

stash BOOKS.

fabric arts for a handmade lifestyle

If you're craving beautiful authenticity in a time of mass-production...Stash Books is for you. Stash Books is a line of how-to books celebrating fabric arts for a handmade lifestyle. Backed by C&T Publishing's solid reputation for quality, Stash Books will inspire you with contemporary designs, clear and simple instructions, and engaging photography.

ctpub.com